Pick another
CHECKOUT LANE,
honey

SAVE **BIG** MONEY &
MAKE THE GROCERY AISLE
YOUR CATWALK!

JOANIE DEMER & HEATHER WHEELER

AVIVA
PUBLISHING
NEW YORK

Pick Another Checkout Lane, Honey
Save BIG Money and Make the Grocery Aisle Your Catwalk!
© 2010 Joanie Demer & Heather Wheeler

Address all inquiries to:
The Krazy Coupon Lady
permissions@thekrazycouponlady.com

PickAnotherCheckOutLaneHoney.com
TheKrazyCouponLady.com

ISBN: 978-0-9841497-8-0

Library of Congress Control Number: 2009938615

Editor: Anonymous writer behind *Seriously So Blessed*
Cartoonist: Hugo Camacho

Printed in United States of America

First Edition

For additional copies visit: PickAnotherCheckOutLaneHoney.com

Dedication

To our awesome kids, nothing brings us joy like you do, not even free detergent.

To our loving husbands, thanks for understanding
every time we disappear to the store for hours longer than promised.

To our parents, thanks for teaching us to work hard and be frugal, and for
never buying that pony we begged for after watching *Wild Hearts Can't be Broken.*

To our readers, thanks for your support and for checking TheKrazyCouponLady.com
more times in a day than you check your kid's diaper.

Oprah and Donald, when this coupon thing catches on and
you want a private lesson, have your people call our people
and we'll see if we can squeeze you onto our calendar.

Contents:

From the Authors

Are we the only people touting coupons as an easy way to save money? Are we deep-pocketed VIPs straight from the Ivy League? Are we scarily smart or especially eloquent? Nope, nope, nope. We're just two motivated, hard-working, stay-at-home moms with a knack for saving piles of cash, here to offer you some tried and true tips that will change the way you do just about everything. The two of us have saved thousands of dollars by using coupons, and we're ready to help you do the same for your family. We've got this down to a science: an addicting, rewarding, entertaining science. Our experiences are sometimes awful, sometimes embarrassing, often hilarious, and this book shares them with you so you too can learn to enjoy paying mere pennies of the retail price on just about everything. We're bold, forward, sassy, and ready to tell it like it is so you'll be prepared for real life. Ready? With our help, you're about to save a ton of money.

When you finish this book, you'll be ready to shop, save, and shock your friends and family with the screamin' deals you get. Never again will you spend four bucks on a box of cereal. Unlike some books that only give you part of the story and make you pay a membership fee for the rest of their info, with this book and our free website (TheKrazyCouponLady.com), you'll be ready to rock, coupon, and roll.

Beginning to coupon is a little like surfing. We're not very talented surfers with loads of experience, but we know how to paddle hard, stand up, and ride the wave. It's the same with coupons. No need to be a math whiz or to spend every second of your free time with fliers and scissors; our methods are simple and can be used by anyone willing to give it a whirl. You don't learn how to surf waiting idly for the perfect wave to carry your lazy rump to shore. You've got to paddle hard and ride the waves as they come. It's the same with couponing: to learn, you've got to jump right in. If you have this book in your hand, you're almost ready to go. Get ready to paddle hard, do the work, and commit to saving big. If you can do that, you'll soon find yourself walking the aisles confidently, smiling as cashiers and people in line behind you gasp in amazement when your total price appears. Before you know it, these couponing methods will come naturally to you, and you'll find yourself up at dawn, itching to go to the store for the next krazy bargain.

One word about the text—throughout this book, we will use "I" to refer to one of our particular experiences or to refer to experiences we've both had. With the exception of a couple of places where we refer to one of us in particular, the stories and savings we describe have typically happened to both of us. We decided to write as if we were one person because we wanted *Pick Another Checkout Lane, Honey* to be a down-to-earth personal book that makes you feel as if you were learning from a friend and actually in the grocery store shopping with us.

If you apply what we teach you, you will easily save at least 50% off your entire grocery bill each month. If you're interested in getting more for less in all aspects of your life, let's do this. Ready to ride this krazy couponing wave with us? Here we go. Visualize success. Picture yourself coupon-confident, with all the skills and tools you need…oh, and a pair of heels.

Frugally yours,

Heather and Joanie

INTRODUCTION

Why Couponing

IS ABOUT TO CHANGE YOUR LIFE

Sometimes, I wear high heels to the grocery store. I strut down the produce aisle and smile at the sharp clickety-clack they make on the cold, square tiles. My coupon binder weighs more than my firstborn (literally!), and it teeters precariously on my shopping cart. I don't coupon because I'm poor. I do it so I can decide where to spend my money instead of letting retail prices decide for me. Couponing makes sense, whether it's to pay off debt, make ends meet, save for a glam family vacation, or to build a stockpile that will have your neighbors wondering whether your new addiction is shoplifting. Whatever the reason, you'll be the talk of the playgroup, and your friends will be beating down your door asking for your trade secrets. Ready to rock your grocery shopping world? I'm here to answer your questions and give you all the inside tips you need, just like any great girlfriend would. And that's what we're about to be: girlfriends, or as I affectionately call us, "krazies." So grab your favorite pillow, curl up somewhere comfy with the last full-priced Diet Coke you'll ever buy, and get ready to throw out everything you know about grocery and retail shopping forever.

Are you ready to learn how to take the reins of your family finances? Could your family use a bit more money each month? Get ready never to pay over a quarter for toothpaste, cake mix, toilet paper, fruit snacks, shampoo, or pasta sauce again. Want to get soap, maxi-pads, salad dressing, barbecue sauce and more for absolutely FREE? How would you like to make money while shopping? We'll show you how you can even get paid through rebates, "stacking" and even doubling your coupons for the items you're already buying every day.

Becoming a Krazy Coupon Lady means more than saving on your groceries. *Pick Another Checkout Lane, Honey* is a new attitude, a way of life. We want you to have all the things about which you've been dreaming, and we're going to show you how you can do it. Once you're saving 80% on your monthly grocery budget, you will have a surplus that you may use to pay down debt or buy that new handbag or chaise you've been eyeing. Our methods are so effective and, dare we say, "krazy," you just might do both.

How do you pronounce 'coupon'?
Koo-pon or Kyoo-pon
Based on results of our poll, half of us say koo-pon and the other half say kyoo-pon. Either pronunciation is correct!

Shopping with coupons has already changed thousands of lives. Here are just few of the hundreds of emails and responses from some of our fellow Krazy Coupon Ladies.

> *I used to hate the feeling of standing at the cash register as (beep after beep) my fate was decided. Now I love watching how high my bill goes before it plummets down the cliff of coupons and Catalinas. As I stand there, I know that I am in control, and that, miracle of miracles, I am more than happy to pay the bottom line. It's a reward for what I do daily. I tell the cash register what is an acceptable amount. I am not his victim. — Sarah*

You can see your grocery savings on your first trip to the store. Listen to what Julie in Knoxville, Tennessee had to say:

> *I've only been at this for two months now, but what a difference it has made. In two months alone, I've been able to purchase $750+ in groceries/supplies for under $350. That's only $175 a month, and that's mostly because I've been stockpiling at the same time; in the months to come I expect to spend less*

because we'll already have much of what we need. My husband was kind of iffy when he saw me putting my binder together and clipping inserts, but now he asks me how we did as soon as I come home from the store—and instead of awaiting "my doom" at the cash register, I'm all smiles when I sign that receipt. Thank you so much!

Is your family budget feeling tight? Have you considered finding more work to supplement your income? Wouldn't it be nice to save hundreds of dollars per month? Krazy Coupon Ladies don't do all this just to save money. We also treat couponing as one big party. You'll quickly feel the coupon buzz, and then you'll be hooked. We'll show you how to get all of this for only a couple of hours a week. It'll be your favorite new hobby. All the scrapbookers, golfers, gym rats, and tennis club gurus pay money for their hobbies, but your new hobby is about to pay YOU.

Another Krazy Coupon Lady wrote in:

Couponing has absolutely CHANGED my life! We always were living paycheck to paycheck, and when we really sat down and looked at where our money was going, we found we were spending $1,400/month on food and other necessities! Yikes! In only six weeks of couponing, I was able to bring that cost down to only $90!!! WOW! I'm hoping my new hobby will allow us to feel a bit more relaxed about our finances. — Sarah R

Don't worry. We're not misers, applauding one another for saving $0.30 on paper towels. We don't buy cases of soup we'll never use just so we can get $0.50 off. Maybe that's your perception of coupon ladies: eager to work hard for a few pennies or nickels. Though I think working to save every penny is respectable, that's not me. I work to find the big coupons, and I use them only when the item I'm buying goes on sale, making the final price mere pennies on the dollar. The difference between a coupon lady and a Krazy Coupon Lady is *when* she uses her coupon. Krazy Coupon Ladies find a sale item and pair that with a coupon. Often, I pay only sales tax because coupons allow me to get the item for free.

Still skeptical? Read on, and let's see whether I can convince you. At first, it might sound too good to be true. I still remember talking to my aunt, who had just returned from a shopping trip where she saved $600, and turning to my husband and saying, "This has gotta be a pyramid scheme." How wrong I was! Look at me now, preaching the couponing gospel to all who will listen.

Are you ready to keep an open mind? This isn't multi-level marketing. I'm not going to ask you for a penny. I'm not selling you a subscription to a website or Krazy Coupon Lady-brand coupons. Everything your mother taught you about shopping is wrong (sorry, Mom). All your perceptions about coupons and those who coupon are probably incorrect. I know what you've been thinking, and I'm here to convince you you've got it all wrong. Get ready to throw everything you thought you knew about coupons out the window! Keep reading and start saving!

Throw everything you thought you knew about couponing out the window.

THINGS YOU THOUGHT YOU KNEW. . .

1. *I can't eat healthy, balanced meals with the kinds of foods the Krazy Coupon Ladies stockpile.*

Wrong! At first glance, you might think you can only find coupons for processed foods. How do you think we Krazy Coupon Ladies stay so trim? Stuffing our frugal faces with mac and cheese by day and Twinkies by night? Come on now. Of course not. Many of the items we receive for free *are* processed foods: macaroni and cheese, granola bars, juice, cereals, etc. But we've also purchased many other items, such as cooking ingredients, spices, and baking staples like oats and sugar. We've even couponed milk, cheese, yogurt, eggs, carrots, bread, pork, chicken, and beef. Sometimes we can find completely free frozen veggies (great for stockpiling) or bagged salads for $0.50 or less. And it's even easier to be healthy when you have more wiggle room in the family budget. Don't worry; you can certainly continue to buy the items you want and mix and match them to fit into your family's diet. Plus, coupons follow American spending patterns, so you'll begin to notice deals on what is currently popular. These days, I can always find coupons for organic, diet and health foods. *Coupons can save you money on many healthy foods.*

2. *I've seen the coupons in the Sunday paper and they aren't for things that I buy.*

Wrong! Be honest. Get your grocery list out. Are you going to buy any of these things any time soon?

- Granola bars, breakfast bars & fruit snacks
- Canned soups and broth
- Breakfast cereal
- Condiments & salad dressing
- Yogurt & other dairy products
- Canned or individual cups of fruit
- Cake and brownie mixes
- Prepared side dishes
- Paper plates and napkins
- Candy

- Frozen dinners, rolls, pizza, veggies & desserts
- Juice
- Foil, plastic bags and containers, trash bags
- Pet food and treats
- Diapers, wipes, baby formula & supplies
- Batteries and lightbulbs
- Laundry detergent and fabric softener
- Make-up
- Dish soap and dishwasher detergent
- Medicine & vitamins
- Lotion and sunscreen
- Soap, body wash, face wash
- Shave gel, razors, and deodorant
- Feminine hygiene products
- Shampoo, conditioner, and styling products
- Toothpaste, toothbrushes, mouthwash, whitening strips
- Surface cleaners: sanitary wipes, bathroom cleaners and more

If someone isn't planning to buy at least one thing on that list, she is one starving, hairy, smelly nutcase. In addition to all the food items to buy with coupons, almost half of all the coupons you'll find in your local Sunday paper are for household items and cleaning supplies. These items are normally quite expensive, but thanks to our krazy couponing ways, we get them for close to free. The best part about getting a good deal on stuff like toiletries, cleaning products and plastic bags is they don't expire for ages. This means you can wait for a rock bottom (or free) price. Purchase two-years worth of dishwashing detergent when they're $0.50 each after sale and coupon, instead of $5.99 and you'll be saving yourself almost $200 over the next two years just by stockpiling one product! *Your Sunday paper contains many valuable coupons for things you already buy all the time.*

3. *It's embarrassing to use coupons.*

Wrong! This is so false it pains my frugal little heart. Coupons are for everyone: guys or gals, living in tidy trailers or Trump towers. They're for any and all smart and savvy people who might like to do something with their money besides happily hand their hard-earned cash to a grocery store. Clipping coupons is becoming the chic way to shop, and you should never feel embarrassed to use them. The manufacturer reimburses the store for every cent of each coupon, plus a handling fee, so use them without shame. Sometimes I think I'm living in a bizarro world: a place where people are paying eight times what I pay for my groceries and everyone calls them normal. Since when does senseless spending make you rational? Seems like we should be called the "sane coupon ladies." The krazy ones are those next to us in line paying $150 for a cartload of groceries. *People of every income level use coupons proudly, and you should never feel embarrassed to do the same.*

4. *It's not worth my time to shop at multiple stores, plus invest all the time it must take to clip and organize coupons.*

Wrong! Yes, using coupons takes some time. Anybody who tells you otherwise is lying and probably wants to steal your coupons. But it doesn't have to take over your life. You can limit your organizing time to about an hour a week and still experience serious saving. Sure, you'll spend more time at the grocery store once you're a Krazy Coupon Lady. Is saving obscene amounts of money worth a few hours? You can be the judge of that. I often think of my old economics teacher explaining the principle "there is no such thing as a free lunch." She would have told me that free groceries aren't actually free, given the time it takes to clip coupons, travel to the store, and do the shopping. But in just a few short hours each week, you'll be reducing your spending by an average of $50-200. Though it may not technically be free, that will definitely buy a lot more than lunch. And even my economics teacher would agree with that, especially on her salary. *Couponing, like any solid investment, takes some time, but we think you'll find it's worth it.*

5. *Buying generic brand products at discount stores or bulk items at wholesale clubs will be cheaper than buying name brand products with coupons.*

Wrong! It's all about TIMING. I'll admit, I used to think store brands were cheaper. I would clip my coupons, make my shopping list based on the meals I was cooking that week, and head to my grocery store. I would look at the coupon for $0.25 off Bounty paper towels, and then look at the price of the store's generic. It was always much cheaper to buy generic, so I would ditch my coupon and grab the store brand towels. I would always leave the store feeling bad for those poor souls who use coupons and don't save a dime. But I had it all wrong! A Krazy Coupon Lady doesn't make her list and buy what's on it regardless of the price. She waits until an item goes on sale and then she "stacks" that sale with a coupon. ("Stacking" means she adds a coupon on top of another coupon and/or sale, so her savings start to "stack" up). But we don't stop there. We take the opportunity to STOCK UP. Ever since I've become a certifiable Krazy Coupon Lady, I can't go into a wholesale club without cringing. Everything I used to buy every month or so now looks ridiculously overpriced. Things like bottled water, barbecue sauce, frozen chicken breasts, soy milk, dish and laundry detergent...I could go on all day. The first time my wholesale club membership was up for renewal, I canceled it and used the money I saved to buy several newspaper subscriptions for coupons. Now all I miss about my old wholesale club is the cheap hot dog and soda combo. *Effective couponing is all about timing. Keep your coupons ready, and use them only with great sales, so you can stockpile at prices much lower than the price of a generic item.*

6. *You shouldn't keep coupons for products you won't use.*

Wrong! Keep them all. It takes a little longer to save and organize them all, but if you throw them out against our best advice, you'll regret it. Keeping and clipping everything allows you to take advantage of every krazy sale that comes along, and sometimes (watch out, this might blow your mind), you can actually make money. Check this out: at Walgreen's a while back, Bayer Blood Glucose Meters were on sale for $25.00. There was a coupon for $25.00 off, which some short-sighted couponers may have tossed thinking they'd never use a blood glucose meter. But those of us who had clipped and organized every coupon were able to make money, because, when we bought one, we received a $10 Register Reward (a coupon that works like cash on your next order). That's $10 in my pocket. Plus, you will look like a saint when you donate the item to your favorite nursing home. Some may think this is silly, but that $10 earned can go toward things your family actually uses—like $10 worth of deodorant or baby wipes, and yes, we have coupons to use with those things too. *When you clip and organize coupons for everything, you'll be ready to take advantage of incredible promotions sans regret.*

7. *You can't save the big money if you don't live in an area with stores that double coupons.*

Wrong! Couponing is not just for people in one part of the country. Opportunities to double your coupons are great but not necessary. I have *never* shopped at a store that doubles coupons regularly, as many do, and I'm about as krazy as a coupon lady comes. Chances are that as you begin learning your local store policies, you may find that a store in your area occasionally doubles coupons. For instance, K-Mart doubles coupons (up to $2.00 in value) on a regular basis. If you're already trying to shop on a budget, the grocery store you currently shop currently shop may not be the store where you can save the most once you start using coupons. The best deals are often found at higher-end stores with specials such as store coupons; "spend $20, save $5 instantly" promotions; or weekly ads with special sales. *Krazy Coupon Ladies always save big, with or without stores that double coupons.*

8. *People who use coupons end up spending more money on products they didn't need in the first place.*

Wrong! When I first started couponing, I didn't see a HUGE drop in my monthly spending. I was spending close to the same amount of money, but I was buying six times the stuff. I was thrilled to be stockpiling items we used daily, like shampoo, conditioner, salad dressing, toothpaste and cereal. After the first few months of couponing I had a one-year supply of many non-perishable items. Even so, my husband began to get fed up as I continued bringing home car loads of toothpaste, soap and lotion. Of course I was paying next to nothing, but I had become so consumed with shopping for these free toiletries, I neglected buying him much of anything to eat. "I can't eat shampoo!" was a complaint I heard more often than I care to admit. But once our stockpile was built up, suddenly my spending plummeted. I regularly spend about $150-$180 each month on groceries, toiletries, cleaning supplies, and produce for my family of four. Are you concerned with spending too much money, especially on things you may not use? If it's an item you don't already use routinely, make it your personal rule not to pay more than $0.10 for the item. *Krazy Coupon Ladies know how to save, which means they never spend money on things they won't use.*

Whew! Now that the myths are busted and you know the truth about couponing, are you ready to get started? Have you decided what to do with all the extra money you're about to save? Make room in your piggy bank and hold on tight.

In the next year, you can save $10,000 on groceries, build a stockpile of food and toiletries that could feed a small army, all while increasing your financial security, assuring your peace of mind in an uncertain economy, and fostering new self-confidence and pride that might just leave you feeling so good you'll be wearing high heels to the grocery store.

SECTION ONE

Making the Change

CHAPTER ONE

Spending Intervention:

PULL IT TOGETHER!

Get ready to change the way you shop, the way you eat, the way you plan meals, and the way you feel about the grocery store. Everything you thought you knew about grocery shopping is about to go out the window. We'll help you avoid all the common pitfalls and set you up for huge savings success. Here are some basics you need to know to be prepared to take control of your family budget.

• •

LEARN WHAT YOU CAN AND CANNOT CONTROL

Most of us can't control the price of groceries. We can't control the economy, we can't control the weather, we can't control our kids (!), and we don't always have total control over our monthly income. Good news: you can control the pants off of your budget. No more lamenting that the price of milk has skyrocketed or that you don't have a grocery store close to your home. Leave the negativity by the wayside and focus on what you CAN control. Make the change: Get your coupons, learn the ropes, and get organized! Then YOU gain control, and you're in the driver's seat. Don't allow the grocery store to tell you what price you'll pay for that loaf of bread or box of cereal. You dictate the price. Does that freak you out? Let's say it again: you dictate the price. Relax! You don't need to start bickering about prices with your cashier in the checkout

Krazy Coupon Ladies set their price
in a socially appropriate way.

lane or start showing up with your chickens and butter churn ready to barter with your grocer. We dictate the prices because we *only* buy items when 1) they are on sale and 2) we have a coupon (or two!). Seriously. The primary trick we krazies know that you don't is that you have to save the coupons from your Sunday paper and *only* use them once the item has gone on sale. It's as simple as that. Soon you'll build a stockpile of food, all bought for a fraction of the retail price. You'll be prepared. You'll be powerful. You'll be ready to take advantage of any sale at any time. You'll be a sharp, thrifty Krazy Coupon Lady who soon has funds to put toward something more exciting than paper towels.

The Krazy Coupon Lady lifestyle will change the way you shop. It will permanently change the way you think about being a consumer. Once you go krazy, you're crazy for life. Every last Krazy Coupon Lady (or Guy!) will shop differently until she is ancient (and she will be living the good life thanks to a posh retirement made possible by dedicated couponification). After your eyes have been opened to the truth about paying retail price, after the cloak is lifted and you finally understand how ridiculous it is to shop any other way, you'll be hooked for good.

Someone you know is likely clipping coupons already, a coupon lady. That's not enough; you're going to become a Krazy Coupon Lady. Don't just use your coupon on a full-priced product at the store. Get multiple coupons, wait for the product to go on sale, and stock up. In the upcoming chapters, we're going to explain, step by step, how to do just that. Not converted yet? Read on! If you are ready to get this frugal show on the road, jump to Chapter 3 for the step-by-step.

This book isn't about saving a quarter on a roll of toilet paper. I save an average of $600-800 per month from all my coupon shopping for my family. Over the period of a year, saving $800 per month totals almost $10,000. Talk about a pay raise! Take a second or two and think about what an extra ten grand could mean for you and your family. This isn't about saving a nickel here and there. We're talking about life-changing sums of money, financial security, and peace of mind...not to mention the audacious attitude and confidence of a Krazy Coupon Lady.

These results won't take you twenty years to achieve. You could be saving 80% at the grocery store within just a few weeks. Here is just one of the thousands of success stories from another Krazy Coupon Lady:

> *I am definitely a changed woman!! I used to spend soooo much money feeding my large family, but not anymore! I've been couponing for just over two months now, and I've finally reached the point where I've got such a large stockpile that I've cut my weekly grocery bill by more than half!! Now I only buy what's on sale and the things we really NEED that week (like produce, dairy, or other perishables). Yes, couponing does take a lot of work, but it's been WELL worth it! I*

love that I've not only been able to cut back significantly on my grocery budget, but that I also have a great food storage as well. THANKS KCL!! — Jennifer

● ●

MAKE TIME

Ready for the honest truth? This will take work. There is no magic potion, no quick fix, no snap-your-fingers-to-a-zippy-tune-and-make-a-wish. Of course you're going to spend more time than you're used to preparing to shop and actually shopping. And you'll also save more money. We could say that just buying this book and eating some pie will save you thousands, but that would be a big, tasty lie that would get you nowhere. The truth is that you'll need to allocate one to two hours per week to clip and organize coupons and plan shopping trips with the coupon match-ups you'll find at TheKrazyCouponLady.com.

How valuable is your time? If it takes an hour a week to save $800 per month, $200 per hour is absolutely worth my time. The only time I remember effortlessly making money was on each of my birthdays, and my Grandma told me it was because I was very special. Just about everything of value must be earned, and this is no different. While this will take time, you'll find that you really enjoy couponing. The rush you get from saving obscene amounts of money is unlike anything else (although I haven't tried shoplifting, drag racing, or illegal drugs...) Besides the huge savings and the exhilarating high, living frugally is fun. I take pride in knowing that I'm teaching my children to be resourceful and smart shoppers. A few months ago, I received a question while giving a news interview. Someone from the control room asked, "Are your kids embarrassed to shop with you and your coupons?" I responded that my kids are a little young to be embarrassed by anything, including the free chocolate chip cookies smeared all over their faces, but the real answer is ABSOLUTELY NOT. They love to help me with my coupons. Together, we excitedly watch the total drop hundreds at checkout. When they ask for a treat at the store and I say "No," they inevitably ask,

"Do you have a coupon?" They will not remember a time when they had a mother who didn't shop this way. I hope someday I'll be signing them up for their own multiple newspaper subscriptions to be delivered to their college dorms so they can stock up on items for all of their roommates. *Krazy Coupon Ladies set aside a reasonable amount of time each week to organize their coupons and plan their trips. This time is an investment you'll find well worth it.*

LEARN TO SAY "NO"

Once I was shopping a particularly good sale, stocking up on toiletries during a "double coupon" event at a local store. As I recall, I bought about sixty items that day, spending about $5 and saving several hundred dollars. (I told you it was a particularly good sale!) As the kind cashier rang me up, we talked (as we most always do) about my huge savings. The cashier told me how much fun she had watching the Krazy Coupon Ladies come through and get these amazing deals. I asked whether she partook in any of the deals herself, especially since she's already at the store. She told me she "just didn't have the time to coupon." As we chatted, I gave her my best sales pitch, but she insisted that between her job and her family, she just did not have the time to drive around to different stores cashing in on these great deals.

Her refusal to reallocate her time baffles me. How can you not make getting free stuff a priority? "Oh, I think I'll pay for my toothpaste…I don't have time to cut out a tiny piece of paper and get it for free." Of course there are many people (especially parents) who feel totally burnt out and stretched to their limits. The last thing I want to do is add one more thing to the things-mothers-should-do-or-else-feel-guilty-for-not-having-done list. Ooooh, I hate that list.

You are already good enough just how you are. If you decide not to use coupons, that's okay. If you really feel you just don't have the time, you don't need to feel guilty for paying $3 for jam or $4 for cereal. It is your prerogative to allocate your time as you wish. Don't let anyone pressure you into adding this "coupon craze" on your to-do list against your will. As women, we often take on more than we can handle due to feelings of obligation. We're all on an endless quest to do more and be more. There is nothing wrong with taking time to stop, look in the mirror, and tell ourselves we are already good enough.

With couponing, I am confident that any person can fit this into their schedule if they want. For me, it means sometimes staying up past my children's bed time, so that I can run to the store while they are tucked sweetly into their beds. For others, it may mean waking up at the crack of dawn to shop before you head to work, and it often requires loading up your kids for a first hand lesson on economics and social interaction. *Do not be afraid to say, "No," to things for which you really don't have time. If you decide to invest one to two hours a week to save your family money, it may take some creativity, but you can find ways to fit couponing into your schedule.*

· ·

Save Time By Changing the Way You Shop

Once you decide to make the time, you will find that couponing can actually *save* you time in the long run. Remember, in order to become a Krazy Coupon Lady, you must change the way you shop. I can't tell you how often I used to find myself at the grocery store at 4:00 p.m. on a weekday afternoon, grabbing all the necessary ingredients to prepare dinner for my family. With hungry mouths to feed in an hour or two, I'd usually rush around the store, buying whatever I needed regardless of price. I'd often come home with stuff for dinner that night and anything else that caught my eye while at the store. I rationalized my impulsive, expensive ways by remembering food is a need, not a want. Food, shelter, and clothing, right? I've spent years trying to convince my husband that shopping for clothes is a need, but I digress.

Krazy Coupon Ladies get their afternoons back. I *never* run to the store to find something to make for dinner. Thanks to my stockpile, I can just step into my garage and shop on my own shelves. I know the foods I use most often for my family, and I make sure I have plenty on hand at all times. No more wasted time, fuel, and patience making a last-minute run to the store; no more impulse buys, no more fighting rush hour on the way home. And most importantly, the groceries on my shelves at home were purchased at prices far below retail. I often feed my family of four on just a few dollars, including the fresh fruit and a salad. *As you change the way you shop, you will no longer need to make a last-minute run to the grocery store. Krazy Coupon Ladies save time, money, and patience as they build their stockpiles and reclaim their afternoons.*

CHANGE WHERE YOU SHOP

Where you shop can make a huge difference in your savings. There are six main categories of stores to consider when choosing the best places to shop:

1. Supercenters: Shop for your groceries, garden hose, camping tent, school clothes, and new tires all under one roof. Supercenters like to be your one-stop shop. They generally distribute weekly circulars, have regular sale cycles and run limited promotions. The best thing about them? They often match competitor prices, allowing you to do all your coupon shopping in one place. *Examples: Target, Walmart, and Kmart.*

2. Drugstores: Shop for diapers, beauty products, lotions, and sunscreens at drugstores. Drugstores usually have a few aisles of food too. Regular prices are high, but drugstores have some of the most competitive weekly ads around. A Krazy Coupon Lady saves big money, but how would you like to *make* money while shopping? Participate in drugstore rebate programs, and get paid to shop. Each week items are offered cheap or "free after rebate." Add a coupon to one of these "freebates", and it becomes a "moneymaker." *Examples: CVS, Walgreens, and Rite Aid.*

Grocery Stores:

3. No-Frills: I grew up shopping the "no-frills" stores, touted as the everyday low price leader. Here, you'll find shrink-wrapped palates of groceries stacked up to the thirty-foot ceilings. What you won't find is a weekly ad or advertised sale. These no-frills stores are simple: keep costs low and pass along savings to the customer. Without any coupons, this is the cheapest place to shop. If you like to bag your own groceries and save money by buying generics, you've probably already been trolling these aisles. These stores will accept your coupons and can be a good place to shop. Most shoppers only achieve between 20-25% overall grocery savings by shopping solely at a no-frills store.

4. High-End: These supermarkets are often on every corner and are the place you've been using for your late-afternoon shopping runs or for that hot loaf of French bread. You wouldn't do all your shopping here because sometimes prices are even higher than the drugstores. The aisles are clean and wide, the organic section is expansive, and the natural cheeses and olives are tempting. You read the store's large and colorful weekly ad and listen to the radio and television ads, salivating as you hear about all of its gourmet salads and marbled meats for the grill. Everyday prices are sky-high, but sales and gimmicks touting, "Spend $30, receive $15 off your next order" make this the place to stack your coupons with sales and score big.

5. Wholesale Clubs: Free samples are all that's free at the local wholesale club. Seeming as large as the Super Dome, warehouse clubs are the best place to go if you're in the market for a five-pound can of creamed corn. Yearly membership is required to be a patron, usually $40-50 annually. Wholesale clubs can be a good place to shop, but only if you are meticulously careful. I don't necessarily recommend wholesale clubs because they're dangerous! An impulse buy at the grocery store might cost you $3.50, but at a wholesale club, you'll be hard pressed to find an item under $10.00. Many wholesale clubs do not accept manufacturer coupons. Wholesale clubs do tend to have the best consistent prices on milk and eggs. *Examples: Costco, Sam's Club, and BJ's.*

6. Natural Foods: This category includes totally organic grocers, co-ops, natural foods stores, or specialty diet stores. These stores often have the highest prices of all. Fewer of the items in these stores will have coupons, and shopping like the Krazy Coupon Lady at a natural foods store will never get you a cart-load of groceries for under $20, but you can still find big savings. If you're shopping at a natural foods store, you've already made the decision to pay more money to get a premium product. By watching for sales and stacking coupons, you can see a percentage of savings on your monthly grocery budget. Even if you only save 10% on a monthly grocery budget of $500, that's still $50 in your pocket. *Example: Whole Foods*

Got it? Those are the categories. Your new best friend is the local high-end grocery store. Drugstores and Supercenters are the next best thing! If you're like most Krazy Coupon Ladies, once you get started, you'll only visit the "no-frills" stores, wholesale clubs, and natural food stores occasionally. Depending on the stores in your area, you may primarily shop at a Supercenter or even a great drugstore; typically high-end grocery stores will now be your bread and butter, literally. Start watching their weekly ads. Look for sales and promotions, such as "buy 5, save $5" or "spend $25, save $10," buy one get one free offers, and in-ad store coupons. Get ready to set up camp in the high-end's backyard, and watch the savings pour in.

CHANGE THE WAY YOU EAT

I used to make a weekly dinner menu and then shop for the foods on my list. Of course, I'd forget to buy something, so I'd end up running back to the store almost daily for 1-2 items. Now I plan my meals around the foods I have in my stockpile or around items that might be on sale. Recently, my local store had an incredible sale on pork, making it nearly free. I spent the week researching and sharing new pork recipes with my readers. I had never prepared a lot of pork, but I enjoy trying new things. We managed to spice up our lives, while saving a significant amount of money, just by adjusting our eating habits for an exceptional deal. New foods are challenging and fun. I thoroughly enjoy cooking and menu-planning around my stockpile. It's like finally having someone around to answer the eternal question: "What should I make for dinner?" I open my garage or look in the fridge and something new calls out to me. I often used to find myself in a cooking rut; nothing sounded good, and I cooked out of obligation. Even now, sometimes I just don't feel like cooking, but I like having all the food on hand to try something new. *Couponing adds an exciting flexibility and versatility to your diet.*

FIND YOUR BALANCE

Warning: anything this rewarding and fun is going to be addicting. Once you start couponing, it can be difficult to stop. When you walk out the automatic doors with your first full cart of groceries for under $20, you're going to feel that rush, that coupon "high", and you'll want to do it again as soon as possible. Soon you'll nod in agreement when your fellow Krazy Coupon Ladies call coupons a drug. KCL reader Amber wrote in:

> *When I first started couponing, I went nuts! The thought never occurred to me that these sales could happen more than once in a lifetime. After about a month of overdoing it, I was totally burnt out. Now, I realize that most sales*

will be back, and I am able to pace myself and remember that couponing is a marathon, not a sprint. I have found a great couponing routine that works for my family and me. I am not running to the grocery store hourly, and I am still able to save 70% each month on my grocery bill.

When I first started couponing, I was so excited about all the money I was saving, I thought I needed to cash in on EVERY deal at EVERY store. I was shopping at five stores each week: Albertsons, Walgreens, Walmart, Target, and occasionally Kmart. All five, every week. Ridiculous, right? Obviously, it didn't take long before I was completely burnt out. Plus, sometimes my kids would spot the big red bullseye and burst into tears.

You might be a Krazy Coupon Lady if...
an afternoon errand turns into a 4 hour
coupon extravaganza & you still want more!

We can almost guarantee that most beginning Krazy Coupon Ladies will get "carried away." Your husband will joke about the other man in your life—your checker—who sees you more than he does. He'll get frustrated by all the free shampoo you bring home and will try to remind you that he can't eat shampoo. He might even try to verify that you are legitimately buying all of this stuff and not just stuffing it in your purse and high-tailing it out of the store. Rest assured that as soon as you have your stockpile built up, and about the time you can't take anymore harassment from your husband, you won't need to go to the store as often. The ten trips per week will dwindle to five and then to two, and soon life will be back to normal, except with way more room in your budget. *As you get started, find a workable balance with your couponing. Pace yourself, and resist the temptation to let it take over your life.*

SET YOUR PACE

The Coupon Race isn't a sprint. There is no need to dash to every store as fast as you can in an effort to beat other coupon moms. Couponing is not a big conspiracy that's going to be shut down as soon as the stores find out. Your worst enemy will be yourself if you take on too much and become burnt out. Set a pace you can maintain.

If you're a coupon novice, just starting out, we'll refer to you as a "coupon virgin." It's best for coupon virgins to learn one store at a time. You will be way too overwhelmed if you are trying to learn every store policy all at once. Decide on one store where you would like to get krazy, and start there.

Remember that good sales come around all the time. When I was a coupon virgin, I didn't realize that the prices I was seeing were not once in a lifetime sales. The industry standard for coupon and sale cycles is three to four months. Instead of buying a two-year supply of salad dressing, just buy enough to get your family by for three to four months. An obvious exception to this rule is for items without an expiration date, like body wash, toilet paper, and shampoo. *Start slowly and find a pace you can maintain. Remember that this is not the only time you'll be able to take advantage of great deals.*

• •

JUST DO IT

There you have it. Are you feeling up for the challenge? Are you ready to jump on board the train of the coupon revolution? Don't set this book down for a week or a month or worse. No excuses. You can absolutely make this work, and you have us to guide you through it. If you're feeling overwhelmed by all of this, grab a friend or two, and make it a party. Make learning, clipping, and shopping a group effort. If your friends aren't interested, just wait a month or so. When you start building your stockpile, they'll come back around asking for your secrets.

- It's time to grow a spine and seize the day.

- It's time to throw everything you know about grocery shopping out the window.

- No more running to the store at 3:00 p.m. everyday to buy what you need for dinner.

- No more making one list every week to buy ingredients for the five meals you are going to cook, regardless of price.

- No more enormous monthly shopping trip where you spend who knows how much and cringe in horror when you hear the total.

- No more running to the store because you are out of toothpaste and Q-tips.

Say goodbye to those days.

Here's what you need to know...

- You will be going to the store a lot, and you will most likely develop a close relationship with certain stores and people who work there.

- You will have a one-year supply of toothpaste, soap, razors, and disinfectant wipes (among other things) before you can blink.

- Before you know it, you'll be saving between 50-90% at the grocery store!

It's all about shopping with coupons while a product is on sale—and STOCKING UP so you don't have to buy something when it's not cheap or free.

Ready to save big money with your new favorite hobby? Ready to be prepared for whatever the future holds? Building a stockpile while reducing your grocery budget by 80% will help you prepare for any uncertainties you may face in the future.

FAQs:

How much time will it really take to clip my coupons?

It's up to you. On any given Sunday, there may be one to four coupon inserts in your local newspaper, sometimes more. Holiday weekend papers carry no inserts at all. I average one hour of time spent each week to clip and organize my coupons. We'll show you how to organize your coupons in Chapter 6. We'll teach you two different methods with two different time constraints, so you can choose the method that best fits your needs. One method requires more time up front and is easier to use, while the other requires less initial work because you file the coupons without even clipping.

Do you REALLY refuse to pay retail?
What percentage off retail do you typically save?

Yes, I really refuse to pay retail most of the time. I always refuse to pay retail in order to build my stockpile. My stockpile is comprised of items I purchase for around 25% of retail value or less (in other words, at least 75% off). I've seen a coupon for just about everything, but even so, I often buy bread, produce, and milk without coupons. I like to think I'm still refusing to pay retail because I know my price points. For example, I will not pay over $0.98 per pound on most fruit: peaches, grapes, strawberries, pears—you name it. If bread is too expensive, I make my own. When eggs are pricey, I'm tempted to get a chicken coop and some hens. Of course, then I come to my senses. No offense if you have a chicken coop. Maybe you could trade me your eggs for some of my extra coupons?

How do I get multiple coupons?

We discuss this in great detail in Chapter 4, but the two main ways to get multiple coupons are to (1) subscribe to multiple copies of your local Sunday newspaper and (2) print coupons directly from the Printable Coupon Database on TheKrazyCouponLady.com.

What if I hate grocery shopping?
Will this ever work for me?

The other day, a friend called and asked me to teach his wife to coupon. When I spoke with her about it, she turned to me, exhausted, and said that between her new (and fourth) baby and her bitter hatred of grocery shopping, couponing would never work for her. Although she has yet to jump in the coupon game, under the right conditions (such as her husband watching the kids a few nights a week so she can learn, prepare, and shop) she could quickly become a happy and successful Krazy Coupon Lady.

If you hate the grocery store, don't despair. We used to hate grocery shopping too, but coupon shopping is nothing like the mindless aisle-weaving you've done before! It's a game, a challenge and the best natural high since exercise—without all the fatigue and body odor. Give it a try, and you just might find yourself hooked after your very first trip.

CHAPTER TWO

From Meltdown to Miracle:

HOW TO ADJUST TO CHANGE

John F. Kennedy, in his 1962 State of the Union Address, said, "The time to repair the roof is when the sun is shining."

The best time to prepare is now! What would happen if your family's income disappeared tomorrow? Do you worry about unforeseen financial burdens like a health crisis or an auto accident? Instead of fearing your financial future, prepare by summoning your fearless inner Krazy Coupon Lady. The sooner you start saving money and building your stockpile, the sooner you'll experience the security and peace of mind that come from knowing you can handle anything that comes your way.

●　●　●　●　●　●　●　●　●　●　●　●　●　●　●　●　●　●　●

JOANIE'S STORY

My family rang in the New Year happily. We were optimistic about the future and had no reason to worry. I lived in a cute little house in the suburbs with my two beautiful children, my husband, and our little beagle, Sadie. I was a couponing whirlwind, creating a stockpile and slashing our family's budget. In January we celebrated our daughter's first birthday. We had just paid off the hospital bills from her birth and some early medical problems, which were now resolved. Our only debt was our home, which we had owned for four years. It was stressful to watch our equity disappear as our home value plummeted with the market, but we didn't worry too much about it because we weren't planning on moving any time soon.

Without warning, my husband lost his job. One day he had a job and the next, he did not, and we suddenly had no income. We stopped all unnecessary expenditures and scrambled to put our house on the market. The thought of selling our first home, the place where I'd brought my babies home, made me physically sick. The equity we'd felt so excited about a few years earlier was gone, and we were heartbroken. Despite our sadness, we gratefully accepted an offer that would barely get us out above water and started to pack up. My husband met with a recruiter for the U.S. Coast Guard and started the process of joining the military. It was at that point we decided we had to sell our dog, Sadie. I can count the number of times I've seen my husband cry (but not at our wedding or the birth of our kids, mind you). But when the new family walked out the door with our dog, he couldn't hold back his tears. How was I supposed to explain to my two-year-old son that his best friend was going away forever? It was a devastating time for our family.

I stayed strong for my family. I had not yet allowed myself to shed a tear or throw a pity party over losing our home, but all of that changed a few days later. My infant daughter started wheezing, and we took her into the doctor only to have an ambulance called immediately because she wasn't getting enough oxygen to her brain. They rushed her to the hospital where we spent the next twenty-four hours on the brink of being admitted to the pediatric intensive care unit. Thanks to many prayers, her condition improved the next day, and four days later, we took our healthy baby girl home. We were grateful that the situation hadn't been worse, but we still faced $15,000 in hospital bills. We had private insurance and received some assistance, but with a high deductible, we still owed almost $10,000 out of our (unemployed) pockets.

My daughter was released two days before we sold our home. We frantically finished packing, threw everything onto a trailer and headed out. In the space of two months, my family lost our income, sold our house, sold our dog, incurred $15,000 in unexpected hospital bills, moved in with the in-laws and then finally, our kids said goodbye to their daddy for two months while he went to military boot camp. I was left alone with my two children, wondering what had happened to my life.

I'm not sharing this story for sympathy or to throw a pity party. I'm sharing this story to tell you how much security my stockpile provided and how my couponing skills and experience helped keep me from panicking during this time of vulnerability. One month after my husband returned from boot camp, our medical bills were entirely paid off. I stopped all unnecessary spending and lived off of our stockpile of groceries. My grocery expenses over four months totaled less than $150 for a family of four. I had a good stockpile of milk, cheese, chicken, and veggies in my freezer in addition to all my packaged foods. The money bought our perishables like fruit and bread, but you won't believe this: I continued to replenish my stockpile. I only bought things that were under a quarter or totally free. For four months, I didn't have to spend a penny on toilet paper, shampoo, diapers, wipes, crackers, snacks, candy, or baking staples.

Now that I know it's possible to live on so little, our family lives without fear of the unknown financial future. Whatever comes my way, I'm ready to handle it. *Krazy Coupon Ladies don't need to fear the future; because of their stockpiles and frugal habits, they are prepared for anything and enjoy feeling secure in the face of uncertainty.*

PREPARING FOR YOUR RAINY DAY

Some of you are probably interested in couponing because of an unexpected financial downturn in your life. Maybe you haven't had a chance to build your stockpile. Perhaps you have bills to pay and not enough income with which to pay them. Whoever you are and wherever you are on the financial spectrum, the time to start is NOW. Today. Seriously. You can cut your grocery bills in half by using the Krazy Coupon Lady's methods. After you have developed your stockpile (usually within two to three months), you will see your total grocery expenditures drop by 70-80%. Individual shopping trips may yield savings of over 90%.

Take a look at Amber's story:

Coupons changed my life before I ever started using them! Last year my husband had a "mid-life crisis" (at twenty-eight). I suddenly found myself a single

mom to three kids. As if that were not hard enough, my youngest is medically fragile. She has had fifteen surgeries in two years, and has spent a year's worth of days in the hospital. We owe more in medical debt than the value of our home, and the light of day seems far away sometimes.

I was in complete shock and was in a panic about how I was to provide for these kids, keep them in a house, with my unsteady income from my job as a photographer. And then a friend of mine showed up on my doorstep with a near laundry basket sized load of cleaning supplies and food. I tried to pay her for it and she simply said...Why? I got most of it for free. I thought for sure that she was trying to make me feel better, but I would later learn that she was serious.

I can remember coming home from my daughter's first open heart surgery. Our bank account was overdrawn, our credit cards were maxed out, and we had a few spoiled items in the fridge. We had nothing to feed our kids. I remember how I felt like a complete failure.

I have only been seriously stockpiling for 2-3 months now, but in that time, we have been able to keep our food budget to $50/week, and we are gradually chipping away at our debt. Moreover, my kids will never be hungry again. No matter how long we are hospitalized now, I know I can come home to a fully stocked freezer with meats and cheeses, cereal (brand name at that!), rice, and pastas in the perishables pantry...and I know that I can provide for them, even if I had bought nothing else...for at least a month.

I am so thankful for coupons. My husband is home now (thanks to some amazing prayer warriors), and we are enjoying date night—couponing together. Coupons have inspired me, lifted my spirits, provided for my family, and have helped my husband and me bond again. Coupons are so much more to me than a few bucks saved.

We hear dozens of these stories every month: lives transformed by nothing more than strategic shopping with coupons. Financial problems can eat away at your security and your marriage. Those who learn quickly how to restructure their budgets and cash in on these huge savings are experiencing a total financial makeover. *No matter your situation, saving money by using coupons will relieve stress and allow you to breathe more easily.*

● ●

WHERE ARE MY BOOTSTRAPS?

Murphy's Law states, "Anything that can go wrong, will go wrong." Although that's a bit pessimistic for my taste, we all face many unexpected bumps in the road. Perhaps we would do better to expect them. Times that require the greatest flexibility are those we cannot see coming. Save some money, build a stockpile, buy insurance, learn CPR, and always carry an Advil and extra tampon in your purse.

Nearly 170 years ago in 1841, the *Huron Reflector* newspaper printed this poem:

I never had a slice of bread,
Particularly large and wide,
That did not fall upon the floor,
And always on the buttered side.

I had to learn to smile and laugh at my sad predicament this last year, just like I have to laugh when my toast drops buttered side down. I really have nothing to be upset about with my life or my toast. The most important things in my life—the people I love—are here with me now. But I know the importance of preparing for the future, and that's why you will find me in the store on any given day, continuing to build my stockpile for the next rainy day.

Terri shared the same feeling with us:

I started couponing a few months ago. At first it was just something fun to do with a few friends who were also into it. We were going along nicely, getting great deals and building a stockpile of personal care items and foods when my husband was laid off (his second layoff within eight months). Like a lot of people, we are underwater on our house, and there are no jobs out there in his industry. We are so grateful to have enough stored away only to have to purchase staple items like milk and bread on a weekly basis. Couponing has literally helped us survive this trying time. Even with our drastically reduced income, I am still able to take piles of change to the grocery store and continue building our stockpile. I will never stop couponing!!! Thankfully, we were pre-pared when a financial hardship came up. If it weren't for that, we'd probably be using credit cards to buy our groceries, putting us even further into debt.

Don't wait for a crisis to motivate you. Now is the perfect time to start couponing and building your stockpile of food and toiletries. Don't wait for a traumatic event to be your wake-up call or for a tragedy to motivate you to prepare. Don't put off for tomorrow what you can do today. Buy your umbrella before it starts pouring. Luck favors the prepared. How many more cliches do you need me to list before you're ready to climb on the Krazy Coupon Lady bandwagon?

FAQs:

What if I'm already standing in a downpour? What if my rainy day is here right now?

You can begin couponing with little to no cost, and you will see immediate results. If you have no money, you can find everything you need to get started—including coupons—without paying a cent. TheKrazyCouponLady.com is always free and many Krazy Coupon Ladies get extra coupons from neighbors, family members, or convenience store owners before they toss them out. If you are behind on credit card payments, if you don't know where your next house payment is going to come from, if you are unemployed, now is the time to begin couponing.

How much do you suggest stockpiling?

We suggest:

A two-week supply of milk, eggs, and bread.

A one- to two-month supply of perishables that can be frozen, such as meat, cheese, berries, grapes, etc.

Six months or more of edible non-perishables, such as canned goods, drinks, packaged food like applesauce, crackers, cereal, etc.

One to two years of non-perishables, such as laundry detergent, dishwasher detergent, cleaning supplies, toiletries, etc.

Call me krazy, but I personally try to keep a one-year supply of all my food items. It is a decision that my family made together, and we have the room to do it. When possible, stockpile as much as you can use before the expiration date. The larger your stockpile, the less you will be buying each week for your family's immediate needs. Krazy Coupon Ladies save money by buying things *before* they need them.

How long could you comfortably survive on your stockpile?

I could comfortably feed my family for about two months. The things we'd miss the most would be milk and eggs. I have dry milk powder, but it doesn't taste very good. I would start to add more beans to stretch my meats further, but I think we could almost get by without my husband noticing for two months. If I had access to fresh produce, milk and eggs, I could last comfortably for a full six months. Doesn't that security sound wonderful?

CHAPTER THREE

Beat the Joneses!
BUILD A STOCKPILE THAT WILL PUT YOUR NEIGHBORS TO SHAME

My grandmother has always clipped coupons the old-fashioned way. She pulls the coupon inserts from her Sunday paper and clips the coupons she wants. During the following week, she uses those coupons, just like the manufacturer hopes she will. Grandma is a coupon lady, but I'm a Krazy Coupon Lady. Grandma saves a quarter here and there, or a dollar if she's lucky, but I save hundreds each week. What's the difference? Krazy Coupon Ladies like me get multiple copies of the Sunday paper—we're talking about four to six papers per week. Does that sound krazy to you? Here's an example: since I get six copies of the paper, I also get six Skippy peanut butter coupons and file them away (more on that in Chapter 6). Then, when the peanut butter goes on sale and ends up free after the coupon, I just stockpiled a six-month supply. Couponing without stockpiling is like cooking without eating. Couponing without stockpiling is like painting your living room with your makeup brush. It's like trying to mow your lawn by pulling out fistfuls of grass. It's like watering your garden with a baby bottle. You CAN, but it's inconvenient and not worth the time, especially when there's a better way.

A *stockpile* is the stash of food and toiletries that you collect over time. Your stockpile might be in your garage, your basement, your pantry, anywhere you can store your extra food. During a recent move, my stockpile even spent some time in a storage unit.

It doesn't matter where you keep it; the important thing is that you have it.

Why Create A Stockpile?

To save money (and have more cash to spend however you want!)

Spend a little now to save a lot later. I stockpile for the extra zeros it adds to my bank account balance. To pay for your children's education, to pay off debt, to donate to your favorite charity, to hire a cleaning lady, or for the cruise you've been eyeing but can't quite justify yet...whatever it's for, saving hundreds of dollars per month lets you do whatever you want with the extra cash. Believe me, you can't afford NOT to stockpile.

It may sound counter-intuitive that buying and accumulating all this stuff is going to save you money, but soon you'll be a believer. When shopping with coupons, you'll be able to start building your stockpile without spending any more than you're already spending right now. In fact, you might even start spending less right from the start, even while you're packing tons of food and toiletries away for later. Within a few months, you can see overall savings of 60-80%, and your stockpile can be created entirely by items purchased for around 25% of the retail price (in other words, 75% off).

The only way to save the big bucks is to *buy in large quantities when you have coupons AND when it's on sale.* Stockpiling is buying a lot at once, but not necessarily jumbo-sized products. Because of coupons, you'll have many opportunities to stockpile greater quantities of small containers instead of fewer large items. For example, I might buy four 16-ounce jars of peanut butter instead of the big 64-ounce tub. I still look at the price per ounce, but when you add coupons into the mix it makes the smaller items the cheapest. Here's an example.

Store Prices:
64 oz peanut butter is $6.98 ($0.11 per ounce)
16 oz peanut butter is $2.00 ($0.125 per ounce)

With a coupon for $1.00/1 peanut butter, look what happens to the price per ounce.

Final Prices after coupon:

64 oz peanut butter: now $5.98 after coupon = $0.09 per ounce

16 oz peanut butter: now $1.00 after coupon = $0.06 per ounce

See what I mean? The smaller container of peanut butter started out with a higher price per ounce at retail price, but once you factor in your coupons, the smaller size is a much better deal. Stock up when products are free or at a rock-bottom price and avoid running to the store at 8 p.m. when you realize it's your toddler's bedtime, and there's not a single diaper in the house (true story). Maintaining a great stockpile doesn't just save you money; having food and other supplies on hand helps prepare you for just about anything.

IN CASE OF CATASTROPHE

No one likes to think about it, but these disasters do happen, and unless you've been living in a bubble then you know exactly what I'm talking about. Hurricanes, tornadoes, droughts, earthquakes, floods, tsunamis, wars—these all happen, often to people who once watched the news comfortably from their couches and said, "Poor folks; hope they're okay. Glad something like that will never happen to me." A few shelves in your pantry and a few more shelving units in the garage with non-perishable food will go a long way in the event of a big emergency. I'm no paranoid end-of-the-world naysayer, but I'll be darned if I'm going to let that crazy guy with the sign out on the street corner get the last laugh when I don't have food on hand in case of an emergency. If an earthquake comes along and we're stuck, I'd like to be able to break out a picnic for my neighbors that will last us all a few weeks until the helicopters airlift us outta there (assuming my house is still standing and we're all above sea level). Maybe I'd just sell toilet paper for $10 a roll…I'd be rich!

But seriously, Krazy Coupon Ladies are strong and independent. We want to be totally self-sufficient. We hope we can help others, but we certainly won't be counting on anyone else taking care of us in time of crisis. Recent disasters are good reminders that we should be able to depend on ourselves if infrastructure fails and the government is unable to help everyone quickly.

IN CASE FOOD PRICES BEGIN TO FLUCTUATE

There are many unpredictable problems that can affect the price and availability of food. If a new bacteria emerges and kills crops, if an illness sickens or kills livestock, if the demand for fruits and veggies skyrockets and their prices get insanely high, whatever happens, you won't regret having food on hand. We've already seen dairy prices fluctuate dramatically. Nowadays, when a two-pound block of Tillamook cheese goes on sale for $3.99, I buy a cartload and stuff my freezer with them. When you're prepared, there's no need to panic.

IN CASE GAS PRICES GO THROUGH THE ROOF

The price of oil directly affects the price of groceries. The more it costs to transport groceries, the more you'll have to pay to get them. The shipping and oil industries are often unpredictable, so it's comforting to have a stockpile. If truckers go on strike, if gasoline prices quadruple, you can insulate yourself from the effects by having a stockpile. It's nice to think that if gas prices jumped to $15 per gallon tomorrow, I wouldn't have to drive to the store twice a week for overpriced cereal. I could just walk out to my garage and congratulate myself for stocking up when boxes of cereal were $0.50 each.

. . . .

In Case of Job Loss

In any economy, job security is always relative. If you lose your job or someone you depend on is out of work, a stockpile of food will take care of your family's first need. You will be able to save money, to keep making your mortgage payment, fly to job interviews, and keep your head above water instead of spending your savings to feed your family.

While many people are losing their jobs, many more are experiencing pay cuts. Maybe you still have a job, but your hours have been cut. Perhaps you work for commission and have watched your paychecks shrink in recent months. Whatever your individual case may be, millions of employed Americans are adjusting to pay cuts. Could your family survive a 20% pay cut? Before I started couponing, a 20% decrease in monthly income would have crippled our family. Now, we would still notice the difference, but we have enough food in our stockpile that we could cut our grocery spending to make room in the budget.

. . . .

For the Spontaneous Cook Inside You

Having a stockpile allows you to cook what you want without running to the store because you're out of eggs. At 11:00 at night, when the urge hits me to whip up a quick red velvet cake for the neighborhood association meeting in the morning, (or a double batch of chocolate chip cookie dough to binge on in secret), I'm glad I have the ingredients on hand in my perfectly stocked cupboards.

. . . .

For Peace of Mind

Essentially, creating a stockpile is all about peace of mind. One KCL reader wrote:

I used to hate grocery shopping. I thought it was silly to spend so much money on items that were consumable. A year ago I was challenged to live a week on what I had to eat in my home, no grocery shopping, and there was no warning, no last minute run to the store to stock up. My family survived; we got creative with meals, and we snacked less. We ran out of a few things, like flour. And I decided right then that it was time to improve on my food storage. Couponing has allowed me to do that. It has given me the ability to be prepared, at a price I could afford. In January of this year I was laid off from my job. This would've been a much scarier prospect if we had not been prepared. Our grocery budget was already down to a very affordable level. We were able to live on what we had already accumulated and continue to grow our supply. I coupon shop for peace of mind. — Britanie

What price can you put on peace of mind? Telling fear and anxiety to hit the road and knowing you're prepared for the future is one of the best feelings in the world. Luckily, The Krazy Coupon Lady is about to teach you to do it without spending an extra cent. Just a few hours of time each week and you'll be hooked on the safest ephedra-free drug around: couponing!

● ●

FOR OUT-DOING YOUR NEIGHBORS, OF COURSE!

And the last and most important reason to create a life sustaining, budget saving supply of food? To out-stockpile your friends and neighbors, of course! While others are lowering their garage doors to hide their messes, you'll be "accidentally" leaving yours up to showcase your sleek rows of cans, stacks of cereal, and if you're like me, a label for every category. Don't forget to keep your cans dusted! You don't want anything unsightly when you parade your friends into your house through the garage just so you can hear them gasp in awe.

And even if you aren't quite as competitive as I am, it feels pretty great to know that you're in a position to help those around you in a pinch. If my neighbor's husband loses his job, or if my daughter's teacher gets a serious illness, or if anyone I know is in need, I can provide meals or toilet paper or whatever else for literally pennies. And when you help someone with a box or two of supplies, they don't have to feel bad accepting it because you can tell them you got it all for free or a quarter!

We needn't dwell on all the "what if's," but wouldn't it make you feel better to know that you have food on hand to feed your family? What if you could keep them nourished and clean for three months? What about six months? It's why they call me "krazy"; I have a stockpile to last a whole year, and the best part is that I created this one-year stockpile in six months, all without increasing my grocery budget by a cent!

How to Spot a Rock Bottom Price

People ask me all the time, "How do you know what a 'rock bottom' price is?" As a coupon virgin, you may find it difficult to tell the difference between a "meh, just-okay" bargain and a screaming deal. When I first started couponing, I discovered toothpaste for $1.00 per tube. I was used to paying at least $2.50, so I thought I had hit the jackpot. Of course, I bought a bunch of them. Little did I know that Krazy Coupon Ladies buy toothpaste for less than a quarter all the time! Look, if you're completely out of toothpaste and your breath stinks, $1.00 per a tube is great to get you by, but this is *not* the price to use for stocking up. It takes a few trips around the couponing block to figure out what's a good price and what's not.

If you're having trouble spotting a good price, consider making a list of the items you purchase most frequently. Take that list to the superstore where you normally shopped (before you started couponing) and record the prices of these items. Keep it as reference in your coupon binder. As a general rule, if you find a deal that is 75% less than retail, that's a great stockpile price.

Below you will find a sample list of our stock up prices. We have found these prices all over the western United States. Your prices may vary slightly by region, but not as greatly as you might think.

Dairy:

Don't underestimate how much dairy you can stockpile! It's helpful to own a second chest-style freezer to accommodate your stockpile, but that depends on your budget, your space, and your family size. I freeze milk, cheese, butter, and margarine.

My stock up prices:
Whole milk $2.00/gallon

Cheese $3.99/2 lb
Yogurt cups $0.30/each
Butter $1.48/2 lb

Meat:

Don't be afraid of the butcher block at your local grocery store. Talk to your butcher and ask whether he's got any specials on meat. Invariably, he'll have something that is approaching the sell-by date and its price is reduced greatly. *(More on buying meat in Chapter 14).*

With prepackaged meat, watch for the orange discount stickers. Quick quiz: if there is a small package of meat for $2.00 and a larger $6.00 package of the same meat, and they each have a "$1.00 off" orange sticker on the front, which package are you going to buy? *The best price per ounce will again come from the smaller sized package.*

My stock up prices:
Ground beef $1.75/lb
Bone-in beef $1.49/lb
Chicken $1.67/lb
Chicken with bones $1.00/lb

Consumables:

These are items that you'll see coupons for in nearly every Sunday paper. These are just a few of the things Krazy Coupon Ladies can easily stockpile.

My stock up prices:
Cereal $1.00 per box or less
Bisquick $0.90
Granola bars $0.50

Fruit snacks $0.50 or less
Brownie and cookie mixes less than $0.25 or less

Non-food items:

These are the easiest to stockpile for almost nothing. Since they have a longer shelf life than most foods, you can hold out, wait for a screaming deal, and then stock to the rafters. Here are some of the price guidelines to help you know when to do just that.

> My Stock Up Prices:
> Dishwasher tablets $0.75
> Body wash $0.50 or less
> Cleaning supplies (Lysol wipes, bathroom and kitchen cleaners, etc) $0.50 or less
> Chinet paper plates $0.50
> High quality deodorant $0.50
> Dish soap $0.25
> Toothpaste/brushes FREE
> Cheap toilet paper: FREE
> Kotex pads FREE
> Soap FREE
> Cheap deodorant: FREE

STOCKPILING PITFALLS

It is possible to buy too much

Be careful not to buy more than you can use before the product expires. Now that you're all hyped up with visions of barricaded stacks of food that cost you next to nothing, let me offer a few points of caution. With the accessibility and ease of buying forty coupons online (read more about buying coupons online in Chapter 4), it's easy to over-stockpile. The natural coupon high can sometimes lead us astray in this regard. Diligently check expiration dates, and learn how much your family can consume each month. If you overbuy, keep an eye on approaching expiration dates. If you realize you won't be able to use something before it expires, quickly donate your extras to a food bank in your area a month or two before they expire.

Stockpiling a new product

Do NOT stock up on a new product without trying it. I mean it. Even if it's free. Don't do it. I used to buy almost anything if it were free. A single (male) Krazy Coupon Guy bought a bunch of Kotex pads when they were free, just because he could. We brainstormed ideas for alternate Kotex uses: washing windows, band-aids for serious trauma, wiping the dip stick after checking the oil. He turned his free Kotex into a success, but stocking up on a product even if it's free or dirt-cheap can sometimes be a mistake.

I have two young children, both in diapers. Their favorite breakfast is instant oatmeal, and they *each* eat two packets every morning! Breakfast is often the biggest meal of their day because they are at such busy ages where they're on the go all the time. So when I saw a Quaker sale coming up at my local grocery store, I bought an extra forty coupons online (in addition to the coupons I already had from my newspaper subscriptions). The following week I bought two cases: forty-eight boxes of Quaker High Fiber Instant Oatmeal in Maple and Brown Sugar—their favorite flavor! The oatmeal was only $0.25 per box! I was certain this would last my children for at least three months. I was excited to try the "high fiber" variety. We hadn't used it before, but it sounded healthy.

How many of you wise parents have predicted the end of this story? My babies loved the oatmeal, gobbling it up happily. Twelve hours later, I received a fragrant first hand lesson in what fiber does to a small body's digestive system. Thankfully, I was also stocked on diapers and wipes. It was a disaster, and the worst part is I kept feeding it to them. Are you wondering why I didn't immediately stop? Well, because I am stubborn! I figured that maybe their little bodies would adjust to all that good fiber and learn to cope with it. I also started adding bananas in hopes to counteract some of the effects—all to no avail. Now I'm left with a case and a half of high fiber instant oatmeal that we'll never use. Did I mention that I don't like oatmeal? Sure, I'll give away the surplus, but in the end, I'll have spent close to regular price for the boxes we used. All for the oatmeal that my kids loved so much but that didn't love them back. Plus, now I need to start watching diaper sales again to make up for all those extra changes. Is it a good idea to stock up on an unfamiliar product just because it is free or cheap? NO! Always sample the product before buying in bulk.

• •

LET'S TALK LOGISTICS

Creating a stockpile makes good financial sense, even if you make a few oatmeal blunders along the way. Stockpiling is smart even if you never have an emergency. To save big money, you have to buy in multiples. Need an example?

Mandarin Oranges are on sale for $1.00.

I have a "$1.00 off 2" manufacturer coupon and my store is doubling coupons up to a dollar in value.

I can get two cans of free mandarins with one (doubled) coupon, so all I pay is any applicable sales tax.

If I only have one coupon, I'll buy two cans for free, pay the sales tax, and walk out of the store happily. That evening, my family will cheerfully eat both cans of oranges and say, "Wow! Good job saving two dollars!" The following week, I'll make a grocery list and realize we need mandarin oranges. I'll go to the store, this time without any coupons and without the sale price, and buy two more cans of oranges at $1.39 each.

See what happened? If you don't stockpile, you only save $2.00 once. End of story. Getting two cans of free mandarin oranges is not worth the time and effort it takes to clip and organize the coupon in the first place. Think BIG. You need more than one copy of the coupon. Honestly, I like to have at least four copies…sometimes more!

The more copies of each coupon you have, the faster you'll create your stockpile, and the more money you'll save long-term. Krazy Coupon Ladies subscribe to four to six copies of the Sunday paper, and that's just the beginning.

What if I don't have room for a stockpile?
What if I'm living in an apartment?

Everyone's situation will vary. Whatever your circumstances are, make stockpiling a priority. If you live in a tiny apartment, take a look at your closets and see if there's a place you could make room for a shelf or two. You may need to get creative, looking high in the closet, under the bed, maybe even behind the entertainment center. Consider putting in extra shelving or buying free-standing storage units. Don't wait until you have enough room for a one-year supply of food. Just start where you can and reap the savings.

What if I live in a 1-2 person household?
I don't use that much food!

Everyone eats! Even if you live alone, you could benefit from a stockpile. Find the items you eat most often. Maybe it's peanut butter or cream of chicken soup. Maybe it's pickles and potato chips; we won't judge you. Whether you generally cook for one or ten, there are foods you use more than others, and you can save big money. Figure out what you usually buy. When those items go on sale and you have coupons for them, buy a six-month supply.

How am I going to save money at the same time I'm buying way more food?

I know, right?! You'll see what we mean once you get started. For example, right now, without coupons, let's say you buy $10 worth of cereal every two weeks. You get two to three boxes of your favorite cereal and gobble it up. When you start couponing and find boxes of cereal for $1 each (or less!), you'll come home with 8-12 boxes for the same amount of money you used to spend on three boxes. Did you still spend $10? Yes. But *you got more out of that $10,* because you got two months' worth of cereal instead of two weeks' worth. A rock-bottom retail price is nowhere close to as cheap as a stacked couponing price.

How do you make sure nothing expires?

Your own food rotation system will vary according to your needs, but you'll soon figure out what works best for your situation. When I re-stock my stockpile, I make sure the oldest package, box, or can goes in the front and the newest in the back. It's helpful to write the expiration date on the outside of the package in large bold print, so you can spot it easily when you're throwing together dinner. When you notice expiration dates approaching quickly, you can donate to friends, neighbors, or a food bank.

Why should I buy things in small packaging?
Isn't that wasteful and bad for the environment?

Recycling as much as possible helps reduce the amount of packaging waste. With coupons, smaller items are generally cheaper. A coupon is a fixed value discount; a $1.00 coupon makes a $1.07 pint of ice cream a much better deal than a $2.99 half-gallon. It's simple math. Always remember to reduce waste by recycling all the extra packaging. What's most wasteful of all is needlessly throwing your money out the window.

CHAPTER FOUR

Coupon Fetish:
STARTING YOUR
COUPON COLLECTION

I used to dream of a closet bigger than my master bedroom—sleek wooden hangers, mirrors, track lighting, and a wall of designer shoes. The shoes were perfectly organized by color and occasion (in the dream, of course, I have special "occasions" to attend). The closet dream has been replaced; my head is now filled with coupons, sleekly organized by category. Are you ready for your new hobby? You're about to learn all about how to get your hot little hands on the newest, hippest currency. And remember, a coupon lady clips only the coupons she will use that week, but a Krazy Coupon Lady keeps *every last one*. You'll thank us later.

The Federal Trade Commission estimates that 3,000 companies distribute nearly 330 billion coupons each year. It's not just grumpy penny-pinchers using them either. Some 77% of American households use about 8 billion coupons to save $4.7 billion at grocery stores, reports R. Rommel of the *Milwaukee Journal Sentinel.* So how can you get your piece of that pie?

There are many different types of coupons. Use them all! The bigger your coupon stash, the better your savings will be. This chapter will teach you about the different types of coupons and how they all contribute to your coupon closet. I like to think my coupons are like a hot fudge brownie sundae.

NEWSPAPER COUPONS—THE BROWNIE OF MY SUNDAE

The best way to accumulate coupons is riding around every morning in a messenger bag over the shoulder of your thirteen-year-old paperboy. The Sunday newspaper contains valuable freestanding coupon inserts from a variety of manufacturers and marketing companies. Each week, the paper will include at least one coupon insert, except on holiday weekends. A paper may often have two to three inserts and sometimes as many as five. Procter & Gamble inserts come out once a month, while Smart Source and Red Plum marketing companies have inserts that come out nearly every week. Now that you're ready to become a Krazy Coupon Lady, you'll need several copies of these Sunday inserts. Here's how to get them:

- Subscribe to multiple copies of the Sunday paper in your area. You should be able to do this for $1.00 or less per paper, per week. Call your paper's circulation department and ask what specials they offer for people who would like multiple Sunday papers. Also ask whether their paper carries Smart Source, Red Plum, and Procter & Gamble coupons. Usually the largest paper in your area will distribute the most coupon inserts. Many papers offer a Sunday-only subscription, or at least a weekend-only subscription at a lower price than the full week subscription. Do not pay over $2.00 per week for a subscription because you can buy the paper from a newspaper stand for less than that. I get six copies of the Sunday paper and recommend subscribing to four to six copies if possible. Four to six subscriptions should only cost $16-$25 per month. Since you'll soon save an average of $600-$800 per month, the investment is clearly worth it.

- Ask your family members, neighbors, or co-workers to save their coupon inserts for you. After the rumors spread about your new hobby of extreme couponing, the topic will begin to come up naturally—you'll always be talking about your savings! Perhaps when you find a rock-bottom price on dish soap, you could buy enough to share with a neighbor or take a basketful to work to share. Sharing provides the perfect opportunity to mention, "If you want more free stuff, just save your coupon inserts for me, and these baskets of free goodies will keep appearing." You might have a dozen weekly inserts before you know it.

> **Tip:** Don't use the coupons the week you get them. I carry about three months' worth of coupons around in my coupon binder. The coupons are organized by category or date, and they only come out of the binder when I find a great sale or they expire. Coupons don't need to be used immediately.

- Talk to the managers of your local convenience stores, grocery stores, or coffee shops that sell newspapers and ask what they do with the extra papers they don't sell. Many shop owners will love to have you take the extras off their hands so they don't have to worry about recycling them. The key is to make their lives easier, not harder. Have good, clear communication; always show up when you say you will. Make sure to take the complete copies of the papers and sort out your inserts at home. Just pop in, grab your stack of free papers, thank them, and go.

You might be a Krazy Coupon Lady if...
your idea of date night is casing
neighborhood dumpsters and recycling centers.

- If you're feeling brave, consider leaving your pride in the car and rummaging through a community recycling bin. I've known many savvy ladies who have a regular dumpster where they know they can grab a stack of old Sunday papers each week. Now *that's* krazy!

Buying Coupons Online

At first this may sound strange, but you can actually buy pre-clipped coupons online. Pre-clipped coupons are an easy option if six newspaper subscriptions aren't in your budget, or if you think you don't have time to clip or file all those coupons. Pre-clipped coupons are also great if you're looking to supplement or jumpstart your collection.

Coupon sellers have access to hundreds of coupon inserts, and they've established home businesses to clip and sell these coupons on a number of different websites. Coupons generally sell for a handling fee of $0.10-$0.20 each, and their values range around ten times that much. Buying pre-clipped newspaper manufacturer coupons online is an effective way to build your stockpile quickly.

Some people buy all their coupons online in large mixed lots, but we recommend only buying coupons you know you will use. (An exception: If you decide not to subscribe to the paper, buying pre-clipped lots may be a beneficial substitute.) Watch your local sales closely, and buy coupons that will "stack" with a store sale. Never pay money for coupons unless they'll definitely save you more than you paid. When you see a sale price at your store and find a set of coupons online that will create a good stock-up price, that's the time to buy. To be successful, you'll have to stay ahead on your store's upcoming deals. Find out your favorite supermarket's sale schedule. The first day the store releases its ad (usually Sunday or Wednesday), find the coupons you want to buy and purchase them quickly so they'll arrive before the sale price ends. With a little planning, purchasing coupons online is fun and easy.

Even after you have multiple subscriptions to the paper and you're super-organized, buying coupons online is a great supplemental tool. When I see an especially good sale, I love to buy twenty extra coupons online to build up my stockpile for that item. For example: I often buy $1.00/1 toilet paper coupons because I know the four-packs often go on sale at my local store for 10/$10. I pay as low as $0.10 per coupon, so I'll get twenty of them for $2.00 total. When I take twenty coupons to the store, I bring home twenty 4-packs of toilet paper for a final price or $0.10 (plus tax) per pack. That could be written as under $0.03 per roll, and with around 450 sheets per roll, the cost per wipe is so low you won't need to be stingy with your bum. And if you find your two-year old threw an entire roll into the toilet, you might not kill him. Stockpiling to the ceiling works well for toilet paper, cleaning items, and other non-perishable things.

Be careful when buying items that expire. Always check expiration dates before buying bulk quantities of coupons online to make sure you don't over-stockpile. Just the other week, I found a great sale on tuna. After the sale price, store promo and manufacturer coupon, the final price was only $0.10 each. Before I hit the computer to search for coupons, I visited the store to check the expiration dates of the tuna in stock. Luckily, the tuna didn't expire for two years, so I ordered forty coupons for about $4.00 including shipping! Later that week, I received my coupons in the mail, purchased forty pouches of tuna and shared them with some very grateful family members. Staying on top of your expiration dates is necessary in order to be a successful Krazy Coupon Lady.

My favorite place to buy pre-clipped coupons is on eBay. I can usually purchase approximately twenty $1.00 off coupons for $2.00 including the shipping. It's worth my money because those coupons allow me to save $20 when I purchase the product. So, even after the $2.00 I paid for the coupons, I still save $18. If you live by a store that doubles coupons, you might save twice that.

How to Buy Coupons on eBay

Are you an eBay expert or are you like my mom, still afraid to use your credit card online, worried your identity will be swiped? Whether you're a master of the worldwide web or still trying to figure out those newfangled car phones, here are a few tips to help you get started:

- Start by searching for your coupon. Example: Type in "Huggies Coupons" or "Quaker Coupons." If you're looking for a specific coupon, type something more like "$2.00 off Aveeno Coupon." A variety of results will appear. Some will be "auction-format," where you place a bid and eventually the highest bidder wins, while some results will allow you to purchase it immediately. A 'lot', or group of 10 coupons might have a "Buy it now for $0.99." I'm usually in a hurry to get my coupons, so I often choose the "buy it now" format.

- Once you find a coupon you're interested in, take note of two things:

    (1) the location of the seller. It doesn't always matter, but if you're in a big hurry, you may want to find a seller that isn't on the other side of the country.

    (2) the shipping cost. It's often free or just the price of a postage stamp, but be aware of sellers looking to gouge you on these costs.

- Check your seller's feedback rating. Once you find the coupons you're looking for, click the auction title, which will provide even more detailed info. In the top right hand corner, you'll see the seller's name, the number of transactions completed on eBay, and then their feedback rating. I only buy from sellers with at least 98% feedback.

- Make sure you read the fine print on the coupon. Don't be too hasty and buy what you thought was a $1.00/1 coupon that turns out to be $1.00/2. Make sure the coupon is for the exact variety of product you're looking to buy. Don't accidentally buy a Dove Tahitian Renewal Body Wash coupon when you want to stack it with a sale that includes only Dove Original Body Wash.

- Pay attention to the expiration dates, and do NOT waste your money on coupons you won't use. Only buy coupons in advance that have at least thirty days before they expire. If you're buying for a specific sale price, and you'll use the coupons this week, it's okay if the expiration date is a week away as long as you'll be able to use them in time. Very few stores do accept expired coupons, and for this reason, many coupon sellers offer expired coupons on eBay and elsewhere. Be careful—just because they're for sale doesn't mean they haven't already expired.

- Read carefully when you consider buying mixed coupon lots. Remember, we don't usually encourage you buy these coupon assortments unless you're confident you'll use enough of the coupons to make it worth the expense.

Some Krazy Coupon Ladies find it helpful to buy large assortments of coupons as a way to jump-start their coupon stash when they're just starting out.

- We discourage buying *printable* coupons online, but if you decide to, be careful. Clarify that each coupon has an individual number under the bar code to prove it was not photocopied. Make sure you know where the coupons were printed, and try to print some for yourself before you buy. There are many fraudulent coupons being sold online, and Krazy Coupon Ladies do NOT contribute to fraud. Let's just keep it simple, and don't buy printable coupons online!

- Communicate with the seller. I often email sellers with my questions and special needs, such as, "When will these ship? I need them by Saturday." Sellers are often quick to respond, and then I buy and pay immediately. Note that some sellers guarantee same-day shipping if you pay by 3:00 p.m. When I communicate with the sellers, I've always received my coupons in time for the sale. When I have not communicated with the seller or when I've purchased coupons without reading the fine print, I've been disappointed, but only in myself. If you're careful online, you can save a significant amount of money as you stockpile.

COUPON CLIPPING WEBSITES

There are other websites, such as TheCouponClippers.com or CollectableCoupons.com that offer coupons for around $0.07-$0.40 per coupon. They sometimes have clearance coupons for as low as a penny! The price they charge is generally about 10-15% of the coupon's value. These websites clearly state you are paying for the time and handling of the coupon so as not to breach the legal verbiage on the coupon that reads "may not be transferred". Websites like these are great for those who don't care for eBay, or who are looking for a specific number of coupons. If you are getting ready to shop a variety of sales that all have a limit on the quantity allowed per customer, you can use sites such as TheCouponClippers.com or CollectableCoupons.com to select 1 of each of the coupons you need. Or, let's say you need 4 copies of a dozen different coupons, coupon clipping sites are the perfect place to find them quickly! Both eBay and coupon clipping websites are great resources to build your coupon collection. Check out your online options and find which suits you best.

Special Ordering

Sometimes a store will sell out of the item before your coupons arrive in the mail. One strategy to avoid this problem: ask your store whether it will special-order items for you so you can pick them up on a designated day before the end of the sale period. Here are a few tips on how to do this most effectively:

- After you order your coupons, head to the store to talk to the manager. I always try to place my "special orders" through the same person. Make sure you're doing your best to place your order with a store manager. The last thing you need is some punk teenager (said with all the love in the world—I love punk teenagers, especially when they're my checkers!) who will forget to order it, order the wrong thing, or accidentally put my order out on the shelf when it arrives.

- Write down the name of the manager who helped you, and write down the day and time he or she said you could come get it.

- Don't wait for a phone call. Managers are busy and will rarely remember to call you, even if they say they will. Just head to the store once your coupons arrive and when you know your product will be there.

- If you know stores in your area that are high traffic spots for coupon ladies looking for the same product, try not to place your special order at that krazy store. If possible, choose a store that isn't already as hectic, and call or go in when it's not the peak 5:00 p.m. dinner rush. This way, the employees you deal with won't be too overwhelmed by people buying the same item you are trying to special order. It's also less likely that your order gets mixed up with someone else's or that it will be accidentally put out on the shelf.

- Pre-paying for the items when they're not in the store constitutes fraud. Don't do it. However, you can legally have items ordered in and held if the stores are willing. Special ordering can be a lifesaver! I have only had a problem, once, when a store employee accidentally put my order out on the shelf, and it sold before I got in. The process is usually smooth and easy. Store managers are happy to sell you product in bulk and appreciate that you're not clearing them out to do so.

- Don't feel bad about placing a special order if the store is willing. Manufacturers reimburse the store for the coupon's worth (plus a handling fee to more than cover shipping!) so the stores aren't losing money on you—they're making it!

Phew! Now you know all about newspaper coupons and the many ways to get your hands on them: including subscribing to multiple copies of the Sunday newspaper, buying clipped coupons online and maybe even dumpster diving at your recycling center! Remember, newspaper manufacturer coupons are the brownie in my "hot coupon sundae." They are dense, consistent, and a substantial part of my coupon collection. Just like making a brownie, acquiring or clipping these coupons takes maybe forty-five minutes of work. But these coupons only make up 60% of the coupons I redeem. Before I became the Krazy Coupon Lady, I was unaware of all the other sources for great coupons. I was just eating plain old brownie, without even knowing what I was missing.

PRINTABLE COUPONS & eCOUPONS: THE ICE CREAM

Coupons printed or loaded directly from the Internet (we call them "printable coupons or eCoupons") make up 30% of my total coupon spending. These coupons are the vanilla ice cream scoop melting on my brownie. Printable coupons or eCoupons only take a few seconds to acquire, a quick click (or should I say, scoop?) of the mouse and out they come.

Printable Coupons:

Printable coupons were first distributed in the 1990s; people could easily print them at home and redeem the coupons at their local grocers. They disappeared for a while in 2003, because many fraudulent coupons were distributed and sold through eBay. (See why I tell you not to buy printed coupons online?) Hundreds of stores unknowingly accepted these coupons and lost thousands of dollars. In response, many stores stopped accepting ALL printed coupons. Slowly, over the past five years, nearly all stores are again accepting printable coupons, but with more hesitation and stringent policies to ensure legitimacy.

Where do I find printable coupons?

One of the best features of TheKrazyCouponLady.com is the comprehensive list of current printable coupons. It's the most user-friendly list of its kind, organized and alphabetized by product name. It's never been easier to find all the great, high-value coupons ready to print right from your home computer. The KCL printable coupon database includes coupons from individual manufacturer sites as well as larger marketing sites. The Krazy Coupon Lady's printable coupon database is your one-stop shop for free printable coupons straight from the Internet.

Coupons included on the database look like this.

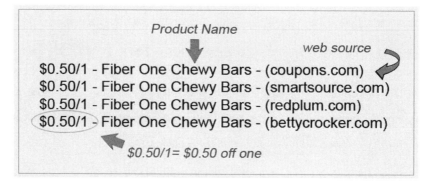

I can't print them all! How do I know when to print?

Now you know where to find printable coupons, many beginners wonder, "Should I print all these coupons now or wait until I need them?"

Here are a few things to take into consideration:

(1) Many coupon offers have a print limit. Once that limit is reached, the campaign is over, and the coupons will no longer be able to print.

(2) Consider the likelihood that you will buy the product for this particular coupon.

When you find a printable coupon, ask yourself:

"Will I be disappointed if I come back to print it, and the offer is over?" If the answer is yes, print it right away.

"Is this for something I buy regularly?" If the answer is yes, print it right away. Often, if you wait until the product is on sale, the coupon will no longer be available to print. Many printable coupons expire thirty days from the day you print, so keep this in mind when deciding whether to give the printer the green light.

People often ask, "Are these printable coupons worth all the ink it takes to print?" Well, only if you redeem the coupons. If you won't use them, try not to print them. And remember, Krazy Coupon Ladies don't pay retail price for ink or paper, either!

Is it worth the ink?

Yes, but change your printer settings to conserve ink. On my computer, I follow these steps to change the setting. (Note that it will stay this way until you change it back.)

1. Go to control panel

2. Click on devices and printers

3. Select which printer you want to adjust

4. Right click on the selected printer and select "*Printing Preferences*"

5. Click on the tab "*Main*", then select "*Fast*" under "*Print Quality*" and check the box next to "*Grayscale*".

eCoupons

Save on ink and avoid a clipping cramp by loading eCoupons straight to your store loyalty card. There are many sites that distribute eCoupons, such as Cellfire, PGeSAVER, Shortcuts, and Upromise. Find links to all your eCoupon sources on TheKrazyCoupon-Lady.com. Load them from your home computer or download them while at the store using your smartphone. eCoupons are the newest wave of coupons to hit the market. They are manufacturer coupons and not suggested to be used in conjuction with other manufacturer coupons, though you may use (or "stack") eCoupons with store coupons. There are three categories of eCoupons:

Save to Card coupons: these are the most common way to save at the grocery store with eCoupons. Load coupons to your supermarket loyalty card, then swipe your card or enter your phone number and see the savings automatically deducted on your receipt.

Target is leading the way with this type of eCoupon. Sign up at Target.com to receive a text message containing Target store coupons and a barcode image that may be scanned at checkout! Hand your cellphone over to the cashier who will scan the image and register the savings when you purchase the items! Additional iPhone apps will soon be showcasing a similar feature.

* *

CATALINA COUPONS: THE HOT FUDGE

Uh oh! We've gone into such detail on newspaper, printable coupons, and eCoupons that this brownie sundae of ours is half-melted, but that's just the way we like it, right? And face it, moms, when was the last time you ate warm toast or finished your cereal before it was soggy? We're used to getting dragged away from what we're doing by all the forces of family and nature combining against us. So, back to the ice cream analogy. Keep the artificially sweetened fruit topping to yourself—my favorite part of my sundae is the hot fudge. I like to let it slide down the edges of the bowl so I can scrape it off the bottom...delicious. Just like the hot fudge is the best part of a sundae, my favorite coupons are called "Catalinas," or checkout coupons.

Never heard of a Catalina? Next time you're at the grocery store, look for a little grey machine attached to the laser scanner at your checkout stand. In all likelihood, you'll see the smart little machine that prints out coupons based on the items you buy. Catalina machines are present in over 23,000 stores in 200 different grocery chains.

You've probably thrown away or left these long receipt-like coupons at the checkout many times before. I used to throw these coupons out without a single glance. Little did I know I was throwing away money. The total value of Catalina coupons and offers printed for customers exceeds 6.5 billion in value each year. Never throw away over 200 million dollars again—it's in poor taste.

Catalina is a giant of a company that now collects information through store loyalty cards on more than 90 million households in nine countries (not bad for a company founded in 1984 by five friends while sailing to Catalina Island off the Southern California coast). Catalina's massive data collection computers access info on more than 250 million transactions every week. Sound a little too much like big brother? Relax. They don't track you by your name; instead each customer is identified by a 40-character number. When I swipe my store loyalty card, the Catalina machine knows the shopping habits attached to my card and the machine prints a relevant ad or coupon. *The Wall Street Journal* published an article on Catalina Marketing Corp in October 2008 and gave an example of how such a transaction would take place:

> GlaxoSmithKline PLC has bought ads for its Tums antacid to target shoppers around holidays like the Fourth of July and Thanksgiving, when they tend to eat more heavily. Catalina serves up the ads to shoppers who have bought Tums in the past. Glaxo found that 60% of shoppers shown the ads come back and buy Tums.

Catalina coupons are redeemed at a rate of over 6%, much higher than the overall newspaper coupon redemption rate of less than 1%. Because of the higher redemption rate, manufacturers pay more to put out a Catalina coupon and in turn, often put out high dollar value savings!

Catalinas can be store or product specific, or sometimes both. Here are the four types of Catalina coupons:

1. **Store-specific coupon:** *Ex.: Save $2 off purchase of any fresh "store brand" meat*

This coupon must be redeemed at the same store (or another location of the same chain store). Other examples of these store Catalinas might be:

$3 off your next produce purchase of $10 or more

$3 off your next purchase of any chicken product

$10 off your next in-store purchase of $60 or more, exclusions such as dairy, tobacco, lottery apply.

2. Store-specific manufacturer coupon: *Ex.: Save $5 off your next shopping order courtesy of General Mills*

These Catalina manufacturer coupons are good on your next shopping order of $5 or more. You'll receive this Catalina by purchasing a minimum dollar amount of specific products. For example, it might say something like, "Spend $25 on participating products and receive $5 off your next order courtesy of Procter & Gamble." Another way to qualify to receive this kind of Catalina is by purchasing a certain number of specific products. For example, "Buy 2 containers of peanut butter and receive $2 off your next shopping order courtesy of Skippy Naturals Peanut Butter."

These Catalinas can be used in conjunction with other manufacturer coupons on a future purchase. Store-specific manufacturer Catalinas can be used on most any products. Exclusions may include dairy, tobacco, lottery items etc. Other examples of these Catalinas might be:

$3 off your next shopping order courtesy of Post Cereals

$10 off your next shopping order courtesy of ConAgra foods

3. Store-AND product-specific manufacturer coupon: *Ex.: Save $2.00 on any Listerine product. Redeem at Walgreens.*

These Catalinas are both product and store specific because they are manufacturer coupons only valid on one product and at one store. Other examples of these store Catalina coupons:

> Free Sobe LifeWater. Redeem at Safeway.
>
> Save $1.00 on any Cottonelle Aloe and E toilet paper. Redeem at Kroger.
>
> Save $4.00 on any one Airwick Freshmatic. Redeem at Albertsons.

4. Non-coupon Catalinas: some Catalinas are just product ads or previews of upcoming promos. These are the ONLY Catalinas you're allowed to throw away!

> When a store promo requires a minimum purchase to receive a Catalina coupon, the minimum purchase amount is almost always *before* coupons and tax. If the minimum purchase is $20 and you spend $19.97, you won't get a Catalina. But if your total is $20.01 before tax and then you use coupons to bring your total down another ten dollars, you *will* receive a Catalina.

What determines the Catalinas that print after my checkout?

Catalinas may be both advertised and unadvertised. Some Catalinas can be counted on and others are generated based on your individual purchase history. Some Catalinas are unadvertised but will consistently work for any customer. It can be a little "hit-and-miss" but because Catalinas are often such high-value coupons, it's generally worth experimenting a little.

Advertised Catalinas that you can count on

Some Catalina promos are printed in the weekly store advertisement. Catalinas are different than other coupons in that they often provide a straight dollar amount off your next purchase. These coupons often print in conjunction with a store promotion, saying something like: "Spend $25 on these 50 participating products and receive a

Catalina good for $10 off your next shopping order." Other examples of advertised Catalinas:

Buy one Degree Deodorant, receive $2.99 off your next shopping order

Buy 5 select juices, receive $5 off your next shopping order

These coupons are usually valid for about two to four weeks after the issue date. Krazy Coupon Ladies know how to maximize these Catalina savings. In the above-mentioned instance: ("Spend $25 on participating products and receive $10 off your next shopping order"), you could buy $100 of products. But instead of buying them in one transaction, I buy them $25 worth of groceries at a time. After my first transaction, I use my $10 off Catalina to offset the cost of my next transaction. Then another Catalina prints and I repeat the process. I am rolling the Catalina from one transaction to the next.

Rolling Catalinas: this refers to the practice of separating your purchase into multiple transactions in order to use register Catalina coupons from your first transaction to pay for your second transaction. Another Catalina prints from the second transaction that pays for the third transaction and so on.

Unadvertised Catalinas

Seemingly Random:

Catalinas sometimes advertise a competitor's brand of the product you just bought. Example: a Skippy ad or coupon will print if you just bought Jif Peanut Butter. Or a Catalina ad might suggest you try a different variety of a product similar to one you just purchased. For instance, if you just bought Kraft Mac and Cheese, it might suggest Kraft single serve Easy Mac Cups.

Catalinas often go by different names at different stores. At Walgreens, for example, they are called Register Rewards. The coupon looks just the same, but it goes by a different name. The store policies surrounding Catalinas also vary.

For example, at Walgreens, you cannot "roll" register rewards from one transaction to the next for the same product. Walgreens' promos often run like this: Buy 1 shave gel, get a $1 Register Reward. If you want to buy three shave gels, here's how you can do it:

Option A: Buy all three together in one transaction and receive one Register Reward coupon for $1 off your next shopping order.

Option B: Buy one shave gel, then receive one Register Reward for $1 off your next shopping order. Buy the second shave gel and use your $1 RR to pay for the shave gel. NO new Register Reward will print.

Option C: Buy each shave gel one at a time and Do NOT roll your register rewards. When all is said and done, you will have three shave gels, which you had to pay for, and three $1 off Register Rewards.

Option C is the smartest choice for Krazy Coupon Ladies who save their coupons to maximize their savings. The following week, when Walgreens runs a Register Reward promo on Breyers ice cream, you can use your three $1 off register rewards from the shave gel to pay for the ice cream and still receive new ice cream register rewards. You *can* "roll" the Register Rewards, just not on the same promotion.

Consistent Unadvertised Catalinas:

Other Catalina promos are unadvertised, but they will work consistently for anyone and get spread through the blogosphere and posted on TheKrazyCouponLady.com. An example of how this works: A KCL reader buys five boxes of Post cereal and receives a $5 Catalina, so she sends an email to KCL; we verify the deal or post it as an "unconfirmed report" and post it for everyone to read. Then others can cash in on the same great deal. Coupon teamwork at its finest! Catalina's new website CouponNetwork. com is beginning to list active Catalina promotions to the public.

Catalina coupons only comprise 5% of the coupons I have on hand, but they definitely provide more than 5% of my total savings. As you begin scoping out the best stores for coupons in your area, keep an eye out for stores that run promos like "Spend $30, get $15 off your next order." These are just fancy words for a Catalina promo. When you "roll" your Catalinas, a "Spend $30, save $15" promo translates to 50% savings before you even use a coupon. This is where it starts getting fun.

A Krazy Coupon Lady steps up to the register and buys just over $30 of groceries and toiletries. Then she hands the cashier her stack of coupons totaling $14 worth of savings. So she only pays $16 plus tax and then receives a Catalina coupon for $15 off her next order. Lather, rinse, repeat! This Krazy Coupon Lady has two more stacks of groceries each totaling just over $30 before coupons! She smiles sweetly and tells the woman getting in line behind her, "Pick another checkout lane, honey," and waits patiently as her cashier rings through the next $30 of groceries. She hands over another stack of coupons totaling $14 worth of savings, and in addition a $15 Catalina coupon and now her total due will be only $1.00 plus tax on the original $30 purchase. That's easily going to be over 90% savings.

Now that we've covered Catalinas, we've discussed 95% of the coupons that most

Krazy Coupon Ladies redeem AND we've got a pretty good looking sundae sitting right before us. We could gobble that sundae up (ignoring calories) and call it good. But it's a sundae, and that means it's time to get fancy. How about the whipped cream, nuts, and the cherry on top? Okay, we may have lost a few of the peanut allergy folks with that one, but stick with this analogy because there are a few more types of coupons that could really spice up your life: blinkies, tear pads, and peelies. I know they sound like awkward college nicknames, but they could save you big bucks, so stick with me.

BLINKIES: THE WHIPPED CREAM

Have you seen those black plastic boxes that hang on the shelf and dispense coupons with a blinking red light? I wish I'd overheard the conversation when they were invented. "What are you gonna call these things?" Surely I would have laughed along when someone said, "Just call it a blinkie!" Or how about the fact that someone came up with those adhesive coupons that peel right off the front of a product and decided to call them "peelies"? We all would have laughed at such a corny concoction. Certainly the blinkie mastermind must have had a better name planned for these little coupons—something a little swankier, like "Catalina." But alas, there's no swanky name, just goofy sounding ones that accurately portray exactly where you can find these coupons.

Smart Source Coupon Machines, otherwise known as "blinkies," may have a ridiculous name, but they also have a high redemption rate, The Smart Source coupon brochure reports redemption at 17% by AC Nielsen/Market Decisions. And with over a billion coupons dispensed each year, that means a whole lot of successfully redeemed coupons. The redemption rate is high because many customers take a blinkie coupon, grab the coordinating product, and redeem it immediately upon checkout that very day. And though we might take blinkies out of the store to put in our binder, we don't take the coupons home if we don't intend to use them. Smart Source Coupon Machines are meant to increase impulse buying, launch a new product or even a counterattack against a competitor's new product. By now you know that Krazy Coupon Ladies do NOT impulse buy, but we utilize every coupon opportunity to its fullest.

Blinkies are manufacturer coupons. The specific coupons and their values vary by location. If you find a blinkie in California, don't expect your auntie in Texas always to find the same great deal in her area. Although blinkie coupons appear in all sorts of different places, they can be used at any store. You don't have to use them at the store where you found them, or even at a store that displays the Smart Source coupon machines. See what I'm saying? You can use them *anywhere*. The blinkie machine is there to disperse manufacturer coupons. The manufacturer is happy to have you take as many as you'll reasonably use! If I see a good coupon in a blinkie machine, I'll often take five of them and place them in my coupon binder. I end up using them maybe two-thirds of the time. Don't flip out...but...sometimes I take them, and then they expire before I can use them. As long as you're not strutting down the aisles, clearing every machine to sell the coupons on eBay, and you're not taking coupons you aren't reasonably likely to use, you're not breaking blinkie etiquette.

If I see a blinkie and I'm aware of a particular sale, sometimes I'll take more than five. Once, for a promo involving Quaker products, I took twenty-five blinkie coupons and used them all on the very same day. Keep in mind that blinkie machines spit out one coupon at a time in about twenty-second intervals. In order to wait for twenty-five coupons to spit out of the machine, you need an attention span that exceeds my own, or a child or husband who likes to carry out special op assignments. Blinkie machines make excellent babysitters for young children, teenagers, and/or husbands. Make the assignment, detail how many coupons you want and let your troops loose in the mine-field of grocery aisle blinkies. The point is that blinkies are free coupons. Don't take them and use them as collage-style gift wrap, but if you think you'll use them, check the expiration date and take a few to add to your stash.

. . . .

TEARPADS: THE NUTS

Tearpads are just like blinkies, but (wait for it...) you tear them off a pad instead of pull-ing them out of a blinkie machine. Just like blinkies, tearpads hang on the aisle right next to a product. It's just a pad of coupons stuck together like a stack of post-it notes. Tearpad etiquette is exactly like blinkie etiquette: take as many as you reasonably believe you will use. Never take the entire pad. I try not to buy tearpad coupons online, because I hate supporting "tearpad stealers" who take the whole pad just to go home and make a few bucks on eBay. Krazy Coupon Ladies don't use tearpad coupons on ev-ery trip, but keep your eyes open. You never know what deal you could stumble onto.

. . . .

PEELIES: THE CHERRY ON TOP

"Pull a peelie, get a dealie, head on home and make a mealie." Peelies are in-your-face manufacturer coupons, trying to get you to buy the brand with the peelie as opposed to its competitor. Like blinkies, peelies vary by region. Watch the expiration dates, as some stores continue to carry products with expired peelies. Peelies are just stickers that can generally be removed from a product and used any time before their expiration dates, but they should be used in good taste. Read the coupon print carefully. If the peelie says, "Save $1 On THIS Box," I won't take it. Note that peelies often contain the word "now," which indicates you can use it on your purchase *now*, as opposed to a future purchase.

Always, always, always read the fine print. For example: A package of string cheese (24-count) had a $2.00 off peelie. But when I read the fine print, the coupon was valid on any package of string cheese six-count or larger. So I peeled off five of the coupons, immediately picked up five smaller packages of string cheese marked at $2.78, and voila! A great deal. Learn the rules and read the fine print so you know all your options.

• •

Manufacturer Coupon Summary

And now we have a magnificent brownie sundae and a handle on various types of coupons. Remember, everything listed above is a manufacturer coupon. No two of these types of coupons may be used together on one product. The only exception to this rule are the Catalina coupons that read "$5 off your next purchase, courtesy of Post Cereals", for example. These flat value-off coupons can be used with other manufacturer coupons. A sample transaction might go like this: Buy 10 boxes of Cheerios at $2.00 each. Use 10 $0.50 off coupons. Your subtotal is now $15.00. You may also use a "Save $10 on your next shopping order" Catalina coupon, bringing your total to $5.00, plus sales tax. It's like paying $0.50 per box. Store coupons (which we cover in more detail below) may be used in addition to manufacturer coupons.

If a coupon reads "one coupon per purchase," it means one manufacturer coupon per purchase of any one item. Many coupon virgins (and some uneducated checkers) think that "purchase" means "transaction." This is not true. "One coupon per purchase" means *per item purchased.* If you have five bottles of shampoo, that is five purchases, even if you pay for them all in the same transaction. You must have five coupons, one for each product. One coupon per purchase is the manufacturer's way of telling you that you cannot use two manufacturer coupons on one item. The cash register is smart, and it will remember how many items you purchased. If you try to use six coupons on five bottles of shampoo the cash register will make an angry beep at the sixth coupon and prompt the cashier to refuse the coupon.

In review: Subscribe to multiple copies of the Sunday paper, as many as you dare. Even if your spouse has to pull out a wheelbarrow to haul them in, your savings will be worth it. Print coupons online and download eCoupons to your store loyalty card. Don't forget to ask your cashier for all those Catalinas you see printing. And never forget to keep your eyes peeled for blinkies, tearpads, and peelies at the grocery store. These are all your manufacturer coupons! Now, on to store coupons.

You might be a Krazy Coupon Lady if. . .

Your husband has to get out a wheelbarrow
to bring in all your Sunday papers.

STORE COUPONS

Many grocery stores have their own store coupons, which you'll be able to find in a few different places. First, stores often publish coupons in their weekly sale circulars. Before you throw away your store ads, browse them for coupons. These ads are often (but not always) available in the store. Second, you may be able to find store coupons on the store's website. For example, Target.com releases new coupons every week. TheKrazyCouponLady.com shares store coupons in "weekly coupon deals" to help you maximize your savings. Target is leading the way, publishing a great deal of store coupons, so always watch your Sunday inserts for coupons with the Target logo. As long as it doesn't say "manufacturer coupon" at the top, it is a store coupon.

A store coupon is basically a discount or price break from the store. The store sacrifices a bit of its price margin to entice you to buy. Note that with manufacturer coupons, stores are reimbursed fully for the coupon's value, but reimbursement usually doesn't take place with store coupons.

"Stacking" (using more than one coupon on the same product) is a fabulous way to save money. Nearly all stores allow you to use both store and manufacturer coupons on one product. Here is an example of how stacking coupons can result in tremendous savings:

Aveeno Baby Products regular price: $3.50
$2.00/1 any Aveeno product (printable manufacturer coupon)
$1.00/1 Aveeno Baby product (Target store coupon)
Final Price: $0.50

FAQs:

Do I save more than I spend printing all these coupons?

Absolutely. The average coupon value is over $1.00 and you can usually print three coupons to a page. Remember to print in grayscale and your savings should exceed your printing cost by a huge margin! TheKrazyCouponLady.com shares deals and coupons on ink and paper. We're always watching for a deal on the things we need and use.

Do you really steal the peelies off the packaging? Isn't that dishonest?

Krazy Coupon Ladies have high ethical standards and don't participate in dishonest or fraudulent couponing. Manufacturers want you to use their coupons to buy their products. If all you're doing is removing one peelie and using it to buy another size of the product (that the coupon does not exclude), you are doing just what the manufacturer intended when they printed the coupon. The coupon is only stuck on the product as a temptation meant to increase impulse buying. Removing peelies may make you squirm at first. The loud ripping sound doesn't help you do it covertly in the store either. Follow your heart, and if it makes you feel like a creep, don't do it. That just leaves more peelies for me.

I see on TheKrazyCouponLady.com that your final prices "reflect Catalina savings." Does that mean I can use the Catalina on the current transaction for immediate savings?

No. Final prices do reflect Catalina savings, but the price is assuming that you are rolling your Catalinas and doing multiple transactions. You will not receive your Catalina coupon until after you've paid. The cashier will hand it to you with your receipt. You may turn around and use it immediately on another purchase.

Can I be a Krazy Coupon Lady and just get one copy of the Sunday paper?

Mmmm, well. . .uh. . .sorta. You can be a successful coupon lady, and you can save money, but you won't see the huge $500 per month or more savings without multiple copies of your Sunday paper. If you choose to supplement with newspaper coupons purchased online or if you live alone and eat very little, then maybe you could be a Krazy Coupon Lady with only one copy. Get creative. You don't necessarily need five subscriptions if you can find friends and family willing to give you their inserts.

Is getting all those Sunday papers wasteful?

Throw away papers or throw away money—the choice is yours. But you can actually find good things to do with your Sunday papers. Some Krazy Coupon Ladies donate to animal shelters or other places always happy to receive extra newspapers. You may have neighbors that would like to read a copy of the Sunday paper. There's nothing wrong with getting your papers, swiping the inserts, and then sharing the newspapers with neighbors or family members.

CHAPTER FIVE

The Barcode's Connected to the Backbone:

ANATOMY OF THE COUPON

Coupons are just ads. They're valuable, but they're still just ads. When a manufacturer changes an existing product, launches a new product, or just needs a little boost, it hires a company to help. Companies like SmartSource and Red Plum create and distribute coupons for the manufacturer's product. The purpose of a coupon is to increase sales, period. It works just about every time, tried and true. It's a simple concept: reduce the price of the item with a coupon and beat your competitors. Create name and brand recognition and get new customers who would not otherwise try your product. The idea is simple and effective, but quite ingenious. Wanna know who came up with it?

Believe it or not, the first coupon was created in 1894. A drugstore owner named Asa Candler bought the formula for Coca-Cola for $2,300. The massive success of the soft drink today is attributed to Candler's innovative marketing, the first of which was...you guessed it...the coupon. Mr. Candler used handwritten tickets that entitled customers to a free bottle of Coca-Cola. Eventually, the drink became a national icon and Candler became the mayor of Atlanta—all proof that good things come from coupons.

The next year, Mr. C.W. Post created a coupon for a penny off his new health cereal—Grape-Nuts. Coupons (and apparently Grape-Nuts) are over a century old! The twentieth century brought the Great Depression and it was then, in the 1930s, that coupons

"Mommy, where do coupons come from?"

". . .when a manufacturer loves his product very, VERY much. . ."

became a staple in many American homes. Coupons allowed families to afford food for their children, and it had never been more important to be a penny pincher. In the 1940s, supermarkets replaced neighborhood grocers, and coupons made the leap. The 1950s saw more than the emergence of cute poodle skirts; the first clearing house was created for sorting and redeeming coupons. In the 1960s, half of American households were clipping coupons. By 1975, some 35 billion coupons were being distributed in the U.S., and 65% of households were using them. Internet printable coupons and online discount codes began to be distributed in the 1990s. And now, in the new millenium, Krazy Coupon Ladies have hit the streets (and the aisles) and thousands of coupon-clipping moms are taking a turn toward the extreme. These new couponing methods are so innovative that I think Asa Candler would be proud!

GREY'S COUPON ANATOMY

Bar Codes

Let's start with the anatomy of a bar code, so you can understand what happens between the cash register and your UPC symbol. Once you have a clear understanding of what the numbers under the barcode mean, you'll be better equipped to deal with any problems at checkout. Misuse of this information or efforts to circumvent the computerized scanner constitute fraudulent coupon use. Grocers, manufacturers and most of all, coupon shoppers will ALL LOSE if we misuse our coupons!

Ready? UPC stands for Universal Product Code. Coupons usually have two of these barcodes. For this bar code education, we'll be referring to the barcode, which looks like this:

A   BBBBB   CCCDD   E

The bar code consists of twelve numbers, represented by letters below: A-BBBBB-CCCDD-E

A: UPC Prefix. This piece of the code will either be a 5 or 9. Some stores offer double coupons: everyday or on certain days of the week, usually slow business dayssuch as Tuesday or Wednesday. Coupons, up to a certain value, often $0.50, will automatically be doubled at the register, making a $0.50 off coupon worth $1.00 off. If you don't have a store that doubles coupons, this first number doesn't matter to you. If the number is a 5, the coupon will be able to be doubled at the register. If the number is a 9, it will not auto-double.

B: Company Prefix. This next portion of the code is called the Company Prefix. These five digits should match the first five digits in the barcode of the item you're going to purchase. It is rare, but sometimes a product on the shelf has the wrong code printed on it. If you are trying to purchase a product and the register is refusing to take the coupon, comparing the coupon's Company Prefix against the product's barcode is the first place to look for a problem. Read the coupon carefully and *make sure* you're abiding by the wording. As long as you're abiding by the wording on the coupon, if the product numbers don't match due to error on the manufacturer's part when coding its product, the store should do an override for you and push the coupon through anyway.

C: Family Code: The second set of five numbers is the family code and value code. Most manufacturers use family codes to separate their products into groups. The number to watch for is the number zero, and more specifically how many zeros there are. If there are three zeros, the coupon is usually meant for any product put out by the brand.

Example Bar Code: 5-17939-**000** any one Method Product

If there are two zeros, the coupon can usually be used on more than one type of product.

Example Bar Code: 5-19200-**300** Lysol Bathroom Cleaner <u>or</u> Mildew Remover or 5-12547-**100** <u>any one</u> Listerine Antiseptic

If there is one zero, the coupon can usually be used on more than one variety or flavor of product.

Example Bar Code: 5-19200-**34<u>0</u>** Lysol Disinfecting Wipes

or 5-12547-**14<u>0</u>** any one Listerine TotalCare Anticavity Mouthwash

If there are no zeros, the coupon is usually meant for one specific product, no variations allowed.

Example Bar Code: 5-192900-**211** Lysol Lemon All Purpose Cleaner Pourable

If the three digit code is a 992, it means the manufacturer doesn't group into families. Because coupons with this code have been abused greatly in the past, many registers are set to "beep" and require the cashier manually to input the value into the register. So if you have trouble with a coupon, and the checker starts to sweat bullets and call over a manager, you might check the family code. If it's a 992, give the checker a little explanation of what that means. Let him know that as long as he verifies that you're buying the correct product, he should go ahead and enter the coupon because it's legitimate.

5-12547-**992** Listerine Whitening Quick Dissolving Strips

As always, there are exceptions to every rule. But generally speaking, this knowledge can be valuable as you shop.

A quick recap: family numbers 000 can usually be used on any product within the family. Family numbers with two zeros apply to most products within the brand, while numbers with one zero work on a few varieties of the same product, and numbers without any zeros usually mean a very specific product. Regardless of what the zeros in the family number allow, the most important thing to remember is that you must abide by the wording of the coupon.

D: Value Code: These two numbers are the value code. These numbers tell the register how much to take off your purchase. If the coupon says "$1.50 off mouthwash," but the value code says 03, the register will only take off $1.10. In this instance, you'd just want to point this problem out to your cashier who should override it and give you $1.50 off, or whatever is stated in the coupon. I rarely look at value codes; I don't find it necessary or worth my time. I just make sure to watch as the cashier rings through my coupons to make sure the correct amount comes off each time.

For your information and education, below are the value numbers and their correlating redemption value.

00 Checker Intervention, Cash Register Beeps, Manual Input Required	33 Buy 2 or more, get $1.00 off	67 $7.50
	34 Buy 2 or more, get $1.25 off	68 $7.00
01 Free Merchandise, Cash Register Beeps, Manual Input Required	35 $0.35	69 $0.69
	36 Buy 2 or more, get $1.50 off	70 $0.70
02 Buy 4 or more, get 1 free	37 Buy 3 or more, get $0.25 off	71 $6.50
03 $1.10	38 Buy 3 or more, get $0.30 off	72 $6.00
04 $1.35	39 $0.39	73 $5.50
05 $1.40	40 $0.40	74 $5.00
06 $1.60	41 Buy 3 or more, get $0.50 off	75 $0.75
07 Buy 3 or more, get $1.50 off	42 Buy 3 or more, get $1.00 off	76 $1.00
08 Buy 2 or more, get $3.00 off	43 Buy 2 or more, get $1.10 off	77 $1.25
09 Buy 3 or more, get $2.00 off	44 Buy 2 or more, get $1.35 off	78 $1.50
10 $0.10	45 $0.45	79 $0.79
11 $1.85	46 Buy 2 or more, get $1.60 off	80 $0.80
12 $0.12	47 Buy 2 or more, get $1.75 off	81 $1.75
13 Buy 4 or more, get $1.00 off	48 Buy 2 or more, get $1.85 off	82 $2.00
14 Buy 1, get 1 free	49 $0.49	83 $2.25
15 $0.15	50 $0.50	84 $2.50
16 Buy 2, get 1 free	51 Buy 2 or more, get $2.00 off	85 $0.85
17 Reserved for Future Use	52 Buy 3 or more, get $0.55 off	86 $2.75
18 $2.60	53 Buy 2 or more, get $0.10 off	87 $3.00
19 Buy 3, get 1 free	54 Buy 2 or more, get $0.15 off	88 $3.25
20 $0.20	55 $0.55	89 $0.89
21 Buy 2 or more, get $0.35 off	56 Buy 2 or more, get $0.20 off	90 $0.90
22 Buy 2 or more, get $0.40 off	57 Buy 2 or more, get $0.25 off	91 $3.50
23 Buy 2 or more, get $0.45 off	58 Buy 2 or more, get $0.30 off	92 $3.75
24 Buy 2 or more, get $0.50 off	59 $0.59	93 $4.00
25 $0.25	60 $0.60	94 Reserved for future use
26 $2.85	61 $10.00	95 $0.95
28 Buy 2, get $0.55 off	62 $9.50	96 $4.50
29 $0.29	63 $9.00	97 Reserved for future use
30 $0.30	64 $8.50	98 Buy 2 or more, get $0.65 off
31 Buy 2 or more, get $0.60 off	65 $0.65	99 $0.99
32 Buy 2 or more, get $0.75 off	66 $8.00	(source: US Application Standard for Coupons)

E: Check digit. You don't need to worry about this digit, just know that it is there to serve as error protection in case of mistyped digits.

• •

PRINTABLE COUPONS

Printable coupons have a barcode just like coupons from the newspaper. Some grocers are still more hesitant about accepting printable coupons for fear they could be fake. Most stores are being re-educated about the differences between fake and legitimate printable coupons. We're about to give you the same education.

One thing that may surprise you: even though you'd never manufacture an illegitimate coupon yourself, if you're not educated and careful, you may unknowingly print and use a fraudulent coupon. To help everyone stay honest and to make sure none of your children end up as property of the state cause Mom's in the slammer, here's the low down on how to spot a legitimate printable coupon and how to weed out a fake.

Things to expect from a legitimate printable coupon:

- Most printable coupons will have an individual code found under the bar code in the top right corner. The numbers will be different on every coupon. This helps cashiers weed out photocopied coupons or other invalid reproductions.

- Most coupons you print online will require you to download software so they can identify your computer and you can print legitimately. So when you are asked to download the coupon printer software from a reputable coupon site, rest assured that it is safe. You can't print without it.

- Most coupons have a print limit, usually one or two prints per computer.

Red Flags that may indicate a fake:

- No expiration date, or expiration date more than a year away.

- Any variation from the standard form/look of a typical printable.

- Unusually high dollar value. If the brand usually puts out coupons between $0.25 and $1.00 and you find one for $4.00 off, that should raise a red flag.

These are general guidelines. As always, there are exceptions to every one of these general rules. If you find a coupon that raises more than one of these red flags, be a skeptic. One of the first tests I perform is to find the source of the coupon. If I can reach the coupon from the manufacturer's home page, I know it is legitimate. Rest assured, when you find a coupon on TheKrazyCouponLady.com, we have run it through the ringer to assure its validity. We've done the grunt work so you can print and save without the worry.

THE COUPON REIMBURSEMENT PROCESS

My two-year-old absolutely loves to hold coupons for me in his sweaty little fists as I peruse the shopping aisles. He loves to hand the coupons to the cashier so they can "go beep." I love that he often gets to watch me shop with just coupons and the change from my purse! But after the cashier scans those sweaty, crumpled, beloved coupons, where do they go?

After I pay, the cashier places the coupons right into her drawer. At the end of her shift, when it's time to count out her till, she will count the coupon values and add them to her total drawer count. The total of the cash and coupon value in her drawer will be calculated to ensure the drawer is accurate. The store manager will collect

Where do coupons go when they die?

Peanut Butter
Coupon funeral.
Jelly was inconsolable.

the week's manufacturer coupons and put them in a pouch to mail, to the store's headquarters or straight to a coupon clearinghouse.

Here's where the real work begins. Over 90% of clearinghouses use Mexican labor. Some use U.S. state prison labor where prisoners count and sort coupons. The clearinghouse is then responsible for sorting through literally millions of coupons. As you can imagine, the variance in size, printing, material, and all the wrinkles in the paper make it necessary to do much of this sorting by hand. Coupons are first sorted by manufacturer. Then, coupons from one manufacturer are placed on a conveyer belt, and a large scanner scans each UPC Bar Code and totals the value of all those coupons. Coupons that are damaged will be sorted out and totaled by hand. Once the clearinghouse has separated and determined the total value of the coupons, they send

the coupons and the invoice with the total due in reimbursement to the manufacturer. Lastly, the manufacturer pays the store back for the amount of the coupon's value, plus shipping and handling.

Manufacturers ask stores to provide "proof of purchase" for nearly all types of coupons. Manufacturers require stores to submit supplier information, product purchase receipts, and product movement reports. Keep in mind that this proof of purchase is from retail stores. Manufacturers want to make sure that the retailer's customers have redeemed the coupons, and the store is not just cutting Sunday Newspaper coupons and submitting them as though redeemed by customers.

Manufacturer coupons provide a handling fee, usually around $0.08, which is simply an additional fee the grocer receives for the trouble of accepting a coupon. If a small grocery store handles, sorts, totals, and invoices the manufacturer on its own, that store keeps the handling fee in addition to the coupon value as reimbursed by the manufacturer. If a store uses a clearinghouse as addressed above, the clearinghouse costs is covered by the handling fee, and the store is reimbursed for the coupon's face value. Some larger grocery stores still get a portion of the handling fee back from the clearinghouse. This whole redemption process takes about a month.

Must I memorize all that bar code information?

No! I don't even have it all memorized. It's just powerful background info to help you understand the interaction between coupons and computers. When a problem arises, you can troubleshoot using this knowledge instead of looking baffled and totally stumped while the cashier types furiously.

What happens if I use a coupon and later find out it was fraudulent?

Consider calling your store's manager, apologizing, and giving him or her a heads up that you found the coupon to be fraudulent. This way the store can avoid accepting more of the fraudulent coupons in the future.

Do stores love coupons or hate them?

Most stores really don't mind. Coupons require more work, but that's why they have the $0.08 handling fee. Some stores like coupons and some don't, but either way, feel confident knowing that stores are reimbursed for the value of every manufacturer coupon you use. You should never be embarrassed when you use legitimate coupons.

CHAPTER SIX

My Other Baby:
How to Build
Your Coupon Binder

Once you get the coupons, deciding how to organize them will make or break your couponing experience. There are many theories on how best to organize your coupons. There's the standard coupon lady. Perhaps she has an envelope or a small plastic accordion file where she keeps her coupons. She only clips and files the coupons she thinks she needs, and once she's at the store, she's constantly realizing she left valuable coupons out or at home. Her method is too small, too unorganized, and too outdated.

And now, a new challenger, for the thousand-dollar-savings-in-a-month fight, weighing in at 12 lbs 9 oz (I told you it weighed more than my first born...), the rookie heavyweight contender! Here is the organized, enormous, heavy, bicep-buildinnnnnggggg... incredible Krazy Coupon Lady Binder!!!!

Honestly, I've tried all the other ways. The Krazy Coupon Lady binder system is the best way to organize your coupons—bar none. I'm so confident you're going to love it, so confident you won't be able to live without it, so confident you'll want to kiss me for showing it to you that I'll give you a money-back guarantee. That's right! Just four monthly installments of $19.99, plus shipping and handling and this incredible system with all its secrets…RRRRRRR…WAIT! Remember how I told you I'm not a salesperson, and I said I wouldn't try to sell you any information? Well, that's why this binder

You might be a
Krazy Coupon Lady if. . .

You catch your husband checking out another
woman's coupon binder, but he assures you,
"yours is better looking than hers."

system is FREE. We're not withholding info or forcing you to fork over extra money to get our tried-and-true tips. We've learned for ourselves what works and we're ready to share the info to help you start saving. Ready?

There are a two different ways to organize your coupon binder. Both have perks and both have drawbacks. It all depends where you want to spend your time. Regardless of which system you choose, you have to separate the pages of your inserts. Here's how you do it:

First, take all the inserts out of all your newspapers. If you have six subscriptions, go through all of the papers and pull out your inserts for the week. Then, separate the inserts by company. Put all the SmartSource inserts together, put all the Red Plum inserts together, put all the Procter & Gamble inserts together, etc. Choose one group to start with and set the others to the side. Go through your first stack of inserts and tear all the pages at the seam until you're left with all single unattached pages. Next, clear off the table and spread the pages of the insert out one by one. Then follow up with the next ripped up insert and create stacks, so you're left with little stacks. If your P&G insert was twelve pages, you'll have twelve stacks, six pages in each stack (because you have six subscriptions). I like to staple each set of pages together. At this point, throw away any ad pages without coupons. There are usually a few pages full of ads toward the back. To spot them, look for something targeting the over-eighty crowd, such as a model in searsucker clamdiggers, polka dot muu-muus, or orthopedic shoes in your choice of five colors. Mark my words: eventually these ads will start to target the younger generations, but for now it's muu-muus and collector plates.

Now it's time to choose one of two different organizing methods: organizing unclipped coupons by date, or clipped coupons by category. I know, I know—choosing teams brings a painful flashback to high school PE, but this is an important decision! Team one spends less time up front and more time right before shopping. Team two spends more time up front and gets to shop hassle free. I'll outline both methods so you can decide which works best for your time and organization strategies.

Method #1: Organize by Date

The basics: file pages of coupon inserts by date, with no clipping.

Supplies

- 200 clear sheet protectors
- 4-5 inch binder
- Tabbed Page Dividers
- Scissors
- 3-ring pencil holder (to hold your scissors)

This method involves less work up front because you spend less time clipping. Once you've separated, sorted, and stapled your ads (as described above), get out a sharpie and write the date of the Sunday the coupons came out on each set of pages. (Tip: find an empty space in the corner to write, as you do NOT want to write across your coupons). Next, place them in sheet protectors and file them in your binder, with the most recent ones in the back. Use tabbed page dividers to separate each week, and be sure to label the divider with the date. Ta-dah! When I outline deals on TheKrazy-CouponLady.com, I'll always tell you the date of the coupon. If your binder is organized by date, this info will allow you to flip right to the page you need, find your coupon and clip it right before you use it. With this method, you don't clip the coupon until you know you're going to use it. Pros: very little time up front. Cons: more time getting ready to go before each individual shopping trip. This makes for the heaviest binder of them all...this is my twelve-pounder!

For this method to work for you, you and your binder need to be best friends and on very familiar terms. Flip through it regularly to see which coupons are nearing their expiration dates. Consider flagging pages with coupons that you want to use before they expire.

Method #2: Organize by Category

The basics: clip the coupons when you get them and file them by category.

Supplies

- 38 - 8 1/2 x 11 sheet protectors

- 3-4" Binder

- 65-75 clear plastic baseball card holders (found at most supercenters, toy stores, or sports memorabilia collector stores)

You will spend an average of forty-five to sixty minutes each week clipping your coupons with this method. If you have multiple copies of the paper, your process will begin just as method #1. Separate all the pages of your inserts and stack them together. Now instead of writing the date, you're ready to get out your scissors. You'll be ready to cut through a stack of six pages at once. The time it takes to clip all the coupons will vary each week, depending on how many inserts you receive on any given Sunday.

Once the coupons are clipped, organize them by category. This is the method most Krazy Coupon Ladies prefer because it takes less last-minute planning before a shopping trip. The categories coordinate with your shopping aisles, and there are one or more categories for each aisle in the store. I love having my coupons organized this way instead of by date. I can go to the grocery store without having planned a specific coupon trip; I just flip through the pages as I shop each aisle. Below are the tested and proven categories I suggest.

Table of Contents

You might be a Krazy Coupon Lady if. . .

Your binder rides in a cart and your baby walks.

At TheKrazyCouponLady.com, you'll find a free download of these binder tabs, ready to print. After you've printed those thirty-seven pages, insert them into the sheet protectors and put them in your binder. Next, insert one baseball card holder sheet behind each category. You'll end up with many sheets of baseball card holders in the refrigerated, freezer, medicine, and surface cleaners sections, just to name a few. You'll find that sometimes your coupons fit nicely into the baseball card holder. Sometimes you'll have to fold them to fit, but it's a helpful way to keep pre-clipped coupons at your fingertips. It's easy to shop spontaneously, browse the clearance sections, or get an unadvertised deal because the coupons are easily organized by category. I love having one clear sheet protector as my very first page, before the Table of Contents. As I shop, I pull coupons from their sleeves and place them in the front pocket until I make it to checkout. You could accomplish the same thing with an envelope or even stuffing them in your bra.

The best part of this method: I don't get frazzled clipping at the grocery store. I'm cool, confident, and my coupons are pre-clipped and ready to rock. It's easy to pull out coupons that have expired to make room for the new ones. My husband is my expired coupon cop. Every week, he goes through my binder and tosses the expired coupons. It's an easy task to delegate—almost as good as the blinkie machine babysitter. The drawback to this method is the additional time it takes to clip everything at the beginning of each week.

In either binder, keep a few blank sleeves to hold store-specific coupons like "$5 off $25 purchase at Rite Aid," or a Catalina coupon for $10 off your next purchase at Albertsons. You'll want to make sure to have room in your binder for drugstore coupons (especially Walgreens or CVS, but we'll share more about specific stores in Chapter 15). Just make sure you have a few empty sleeves on hand so you don't lose these precious bits of paper.

A note of caution: Please put your name and contact information on your coupon binder. I can't tell you how many heart-wrenching stories I've heard from Krazy Coupon Ladies who have lost or left their binders at the store only never to be reunited! My binder is like my third child; sometimes I give it more attention than my other children, and you already know it weighs enough! I would be heartbroken to lose it. Never underestimate the kindness of a stranger who might return your binder to you if there's a name and number to call.

There you have it—two pretty simple and straightforward organizing options. The choice is up to you, so pick whichever method you want. Remember: there isn't a right way or a wrong way. Just find what works for you and perfect it. In a poll of Krazy Coupon Lady readers, those who clipped and organized by category outnumbered those organizing by date by about four to one. If you're on the fence about which method is right for you, you may just want to take the advice of the majority. If you can't stand the thought of clipping all those coupons or worry that you won't have the time, go with the no-clip organizing by date. The trick is to stay organized and make sure you like the method you use. If you dread organizing, you won't use your coupons effectively, and this glorious operation will needlessly fail. It's also key to have a binder that's easy to transport. Nothing is worse than showing up at the store with just a few coupons and running into an unadvertised or clearance sale of which you can't take full advantage!

Once you get the hang of this, it'll be smooth sailing. Just choose the method that sounds most appealing to you and suits your lifestyle. If you give it a try for a few months and find it isn't working for you, switch it up and go another route. We're all different, so one method won't suit everyone. Despite the time it takes to organize, remember that it's "mindless" time so you can easily do it while you watch a movie with your family, or you can get several clipping helpers in on the fun around the table. No need to wait for valuable naptime or a chance to focus (which we all know may never come). However you organize, just make sure it works for you.

FAQs:

Where do I file printable coupons if I organize by date?

If you file by date, buy a few baseball card holders to keep at the front of your binder. As you print coupons from the Internet, clip them and slip them into a baseball card holder right away.

When you organize by category, do you clip every coupon?

No. Sometimes one Sunday insert page has six coupons, all attached, and all six belong in the same section (such as "oral care") and all six expire on the same date. In this case, don't bother cutting them all apart. Just grab an extra 8 1/2 x 11 sheet protector and throw in the entire section of coupons. Every coupon doesn't need to be pre-clipped, as long as they are all in their correct category so you'll know where to find them.

When organizing by date, do you really need 36 Categories?

We've found this way to be the easiest and most effective, but you can certainly change the system to suit your preferences. You could put laundry, dish soap, and cleaning supplies into one category or you could combine soap, hair care, and lotion into one category as well. The categories I have listed are broken down this way to follow the manner in which most stores order their products. In many stores you will find the lotion is by the beauty products and the soap and hair care are entirely in a different part of the store. Try these categories and see what you think. It will be easy to adjust them and customize them as you gain more experience.

CHAPTER SEVEN

Timing is Everything:
HOW AND WHEN
TO USE YOUR COUPONS

A Krazy Coupon Lady doesn't just shop for what she needs *now*. She plans ahead and keeps her savvy eyes peeled for what she *will* need. We are picky shoppers and *never* buy products at full price. We match coupons with sales and promos, we stock up, and we save big! Only use coupons when you can pair them with a sale price, a promotion, or best of all—both.

At any given time, I have around ten to sixteen weeks of coupons stored in my binder. Deciding *when and how* to use all these coupons is what separates the puppies from the big dogs, the pretenders from the contenders, the duds from the divas...the amateur coupon clippers from the Krazy Coupon Ladies.

● ●

TAKE ADVANTAGE OF DOUBLE COUPONS

You've probably heard about stores that "double" coupons, meaning that they accept your coupons at twice the amount of the coupon's face value. While you can still save big without a store that doubles coupons, if you find a doubling promotion, jump on it. Different store policies can vary greatly. Some stores double coupons on a certain day every week, while other stores have a periodic double coupon *week*, advertised in their weekly ad in the Sunday paper. There are even stores that *always* double coupons up to a certain value (usually up to $0.50 off). And lastly, some stores issue a finite number of store coupons that are good for doubling the value of any coupon, up to a specified dollar amount.

If a store doubles coupons up to $1.00 in value, this means that you may present any one coupon valued at $1.00 or less and its value will be doubled. If you use a coupon worth $1.01 off or more, the coupon cannot be doubled. You will receive no extra savings for any coupon worth over $1.00. You with me? During a double coupon period, a $1.00 off coupon is worth the same as a $2.00 off coupon. The $1.00 coupon doubles to $2.00, but a $2.00 coupon will not be doubled.

● ●

KISS GENERICS GOODBYE

Here's a common concern:

"I've tried using coupons, but after I go to all the trouble of clipping, I find that the store generic brand is still cheaper than the name brand with a coupon!"

Not if you time it right! I used to have the same worry. I'd clip my coupons, take them to the store, hunt down the right product and size, do some math in my head and decide it's still cheaper to buy the generic. So I'd grab the generic and toss the coupon... forgive me! Never again!

For example, if you visit your local supermarket to use one "$1 off two cans of cream of chicken soup" coupon, it will end up being cheaper just to buy generic.

Campbell's Cream Soup $1.18
Use $1.00/2 coupon
Final Price: $0.68 each, when you buy 2

Generic Cream Soup: $0.55 each

Tossing the coupon and buying generic is just what a casual coupon clipper would do. But not you! You're on your way to getting krazy, and Krazy Coupon Ladies know better. If you wait and use the coupon when the name brand soups are at a rock-bottom price, OR if you match the coupons with a promotion at your smaller local grocer—*Voila!* Cheap Soup! For example, this week Campbell's soup is on sale for $0.68 cents. Let's do that math!

Campbell's Cream Soup $0.68
Use $1.00/2 coupon
Final Price: $0.18 each, when you buy 2

Now that's a stock-up price! You're saving over 80% on an average retail price and 67% off even the generic price! When someone asks me whether it's cheaper to buy generics than name brand items with coupons, I ask them whether they pay over fifty cents for a box of cereal or twenty cents for a can of soup. That usually answers their question and is the end of their skepticism.

Coupons can only do so much, and by themselves, those little pieces of paper won't change your life. Only you have the power to use your head, get krazy, and unleash the savings potential!

HOW TO SHOP LIKE THE KRAZY COUPON LADY

Step one: Keep an open mind. Don't be afraid to try a new product or a different brand.

One reader, Carolyn, shared this story:

> *Krazy Coupon Lady has helped me learn to branch out! When I grocery shopped before becoming a KCL, I was so stuck in a rut, without even realizing it! I would make my list every two weeks, and it was always the same. Same brands, same size, same meals! Now, I find products that are free and I am given the chance to try them with very little cost out of my pocket.*

I love all the new name brand items I've become accustomed to since using coupons. I don't know how I ever ate generic cereal or baked with generic chocolate chips. I grew up on generics, but now that I've crossed over into greener pastures, it would be hard, nay, impossible ever to go back. How much does generic cereal cost at your grocery store? I bet it's not under $0.50 and that's what I pay for my name brand cereal.

My first baby wore generic diapers. I worried that when he got a rash on his little thighs it was because his mother wasn't spending more money on high quality diapers. I think I paid $0.14 per diaper for size 5 generics, and now I pay less than half of that on name brand. But even after you make the switch from generic to name brand through coupons, you'll get to experiment between brands.

For example, even if you're a loyal Tide lady, if All brand detergent goes on sale for $1.00 per bottle, you may want to consider cheating on your previous brand loyalty. Everyone is allowed one product for which brand they cannot sacrifice. True story: a certain Krazy Coupon husband, Bryan, says he can only tolerate super soft, triple-ply Charmin toilet paper. His KCL wife now brings home cases of cheap, name brand toilet paper she gets for free...the only problem? It's not Charmin. Their family's solution?

Bryan has his own roll of toilet paper in the cupboard and the rest of the family uses the free stuff. This compromise has saved them $5-$10 per month! Bryan and his wife do their best to buy his brand of toilet paper by stacking a coupon with a sale. And, if the toilet paper and coupon constellations ever align and the high end Charmin falls to a rock bottom price, you'd better believe they will be buying every roll they can find.

If you have a brand-loyal family member who, like Bryan, just can't budge, it's okay to have brand loyalty for one product. Just make sure it's not more than one. I was never a very brand loyal person to begin with, but I can't tell you the number of great new products I have brought home since couponing. Products that I never would have looked at twice are now staples in my home. You just might like spicing up your life a little!

Shirk brand loyalty! Take this example: you need laundry detergent. You've been a loyal Tide user all your life. What do you do?

Tide detergent $7.99 per bottle
No sale price
Use your $0.25/1 coupon
Final Price: $7.74

All Small & Mighty Laundry detergent on SALE for $1.99
Use your $1.00/1 All Detergent coupon
Final Price: $0.99 each

Now you'll have to examine your brand loyalty. Go with the best deal!

Another bonus is that coupons allow you to get the newest products at the store. Coupons are often for a brand new product launch! Manufacturers release coupons when launching a new product. The next time your child sees a commercial and shouts, "Mom! I want those crackers shaped like trucks!" or some other newfangled treat on TV, you will very likely say, "Sure! We have coupons for those!" Couponing allows you to try many different new products, so make sure you keep an open mind when finding the best deals. Search by price, not by brand.

Step two: Don't look desperate! One Krazy Coupon Lady's mother-in-law eagerly reported that, upon learning her local store doubled all coupons up to $0.50 in value, spent every single $0.50 coupon she had and "saved a lot." Come on! Don't spend a coupon just because you've got it. Don't spend it because it's about to expire or because it took you ten minutes to successfully find the coordinating product in the store. Save your coupons for when they'll maximize your savings.

If you end up using your coupons just for the sake of redeeming them, the manufacturer will be the only one happy. A week or two later, you'll regret your purchases when you realize you could have found better deals elsewhere. Watch the prices at your grocery store, in the weekly ads and on various couponing websites, including TheKrazyCouponLady.com, of course! Only use your coupons when you are comfortable with the final price. Couponing is all about timing. Just like finding the right time to talk to your husband about his "honey-do" list, or the right time to buy and sell on the stock market, your timing can make or break your couponing success. Be patient. No one wears desperation well. Stay sharp and wait for the right time to buy, then stock up!

Don't use a coupon just because you have it.

Cascade Dishwasher Detergent tabs, 32 ct. $6.49
Use your $0.50/1 coupon
Your store automatically doubles coupons $0.50 and under
Final Price: $5.49 ($0.17 per tab)

Now is NOT the time to buy! Wait for the Cascade to go on sale, or wait for a better coupon. Next week, the smaller 16 count dishwasher tabs may be on sale for $2.49. That's more like it!

Cascade Dishwasher Detergent tabs, 16 ct. $2.49
Use your $0.50/1 coupon

Your store automatically doubles coupons $0.50 and under
Final Price: $1.49 ($0.10-$0.11 per tab)

Step three: Play hard to get. Don't buy a jar of peanut butter just because it's on sale. Krazy Coupon Ladies don't jump on a sale just because it's there. Jumping on a not-so-hot sale or using a coupon just for the sake of using it is exactly what the manufacturer wants you to do, and it will prevent you from saving some krazy cash. Wait for the stars to align. When the sale price matches the coupon, plus stacks with a store coupon and a gift card promo, I like to call it the perfect storm. Well, except that instead of George Clooney sinking his boat, you'll float home happy, basking in savings.

The Perfect Storm

Sale Price + Promo + Coupon

The following is a real life scenario:

Buy 2 Gillette Venus Razors on SALE $6.99

Promo: buy 2, receive $5 off your next order
Use 2 coupons: $4.00/1 Venus Razor
Pay: $5.98 out of pocket, receive $5.00 off your next order
Final Price: $0.98 or $0.49 each when you buy 2 (after factoring your $5 savings on your next order)

Remember, holding out for a great sale and waiting for the perfect storm only applies to building your stockpile. If you're a new coupon virgin, out of peanut butter, and itching for a sammich, find a decent price and go ahead and buy it. When you're shopping for the future, our general rule is to wait until you find a product 75% off after all coupons and discounts. That's the magic number and that's the time to stockpile!

Step four: Remember, grocery prices like to play games. They'll dip up and down by $0.50. Sometimes the store will even turn the tag green as if to signify a screaming deal, when you know it's the same price as the week before. Just ignore the games and pay them no mind. Stay in the zone and you'll be just fine. Grocers and manufacturers are salespeople. Sure, they're not selling you rusty cars, but they're trying to push products by enticing you with big colorful ads that are largely worthless gimmicks. Don't fall prey to their tantalizing, overpriced gourmet foods and their sleek shopping aisles. Don't be fooled by their finely dressed end caps or the sweet snacks at the register.

Bogus Gimmick

Buy 5 Kraft Mac & Cheese, save $1.00!
Kraft Mac & Cheese: $1.19 each
Final Price: $4.95, or $0.99 each

Don't fall victim to gimmicks that aren't any good or a green price tag with a not-so-red-hot price. Remember your bottom line and let the prices and pressures dance around you.

• •

HOW TO GET THINGS FOR FREE

Getting things for free or close to free (often under a quarter!) are common occurrences around TheKrazyCouponLady.com. There are free items every week. And don't worry, it's not shoplifting.

The only thing to note: you will be responsible for sales tax, even when you get the item for free. Uncle Sam is one smart guy. You pay tax on your total *before* coupons. If your total is $10.00 before coupons and you have $8.00 in coupon savings, you're usually responsible for any applicable tax on the $10.00 subtotal.

Don't despair about sales tax. When I say I've saved over 90% on some of my shopping trips, that total includes the sales tax I had to pay. I could actually say I've saved more than 95%! When you get an item for free, sales tax will be all you'll have to pay.

Want to learn how to get things for free?

I'll start with some simple examples:

Kraft BBQ Sauce, sale 10/$10 or $1.00 each

$1.00/1 Kraft BBQ Coupon

Final Price: Free

Kraft BBQ Sauce, sale 10/$10 or $1.00 each

$2.00/2 Kraft BBQ Coupon

Final Price: Free, when you buy 2

NOT free, but pretty close:

Kraft BBQ Sauce, sale 10/$10 or $1.00 each

$1.50/2 Kraft BBQ Coupon

Final Price: $0.50, or $0.25 each when you buy 2

Here's an example of how to get something for free by utilizing an in-store promotion:

Pantene Shampoo on sale this week 3 for $10.00

Catalina Promo: Spend $30 on participating products (including Pantene), receive $12 off your next shopping order

Here's how to get shampoo for free:

Buy 9 bottles of Pantene Shampoo: $30.00

Use 9 $2.00/1 Manufacturer coupons, (let's say I have nine coupons because I ordered some extras online)

Pay: $12.00, or $1.33 per bottle, plus receive $12.00 off my next shopping order

Final Price: FREE after factoring $12 savings off my next shopping order

Did you follow that? The price of Pantene shampoo started at $3.33 per bottle. I then present my $2.00/1 manufacturer coupon, and the price of nine bottles drops to $1.33 per bottle, or $12 total. I pay $12 and receive a $12 coupon off my next shopping order (of any amount). If I had nine more coupons, I could do another identical transaction and use the $12 Catalina coupon to pay for the next set of nine. My out-of-pocket cost (which we sometimes call "OOP," for Out Of Pocket) would be nothing, and I would still receive another Catalina coupon for $12 off my next shopping order.

Want another example of getting something for free? This one involves doubling coupons.

> **ACT Mouthwash, on sale 2/$8.00**
> $2.00/1 Manufacturer Coupon
> Store is doubling all coupons up to $2.00 this week
> *Final Price: FREE*

The price starts at $4.00 per bottle, and when you double your $2.00 off coupon... free mouthwash!

One more scenario:

> **Huggies travel size wipes, regular price $0.97 in the travel size section**
> $1.00/1 Manufacturer Coupon (doesn't specify minimum size)
> *Final Price: FREE*

The manufacturer coupon will usually beep because the $1.00 coupon exceeds the value of the $0.97 product. The cashier should just adjust the price of the coupon down to match the item price (and you can kindly remind the cashier if he or she doesn't know). All you have to pay is tax on the original price. As long as the coupon doesn't exclude trial size or minimum size, you can often get free items in the travel section. You may even be tempted to bust out those itty-bitty shampoos and mouthwashes for every day use!

. . . .

How to Make Money

Make money couponing? I know! You're thinking it's a scam, or you have to stuff envelopes in your living room for pennies a week. Nope. This is legit. Sometimes you can save so much with coupons that the store ends up paying YOU. The best places to make money are drugstores or grocery stores that offer rebates. We will share more about specific drugstore policies in Chapter 15, but for starters, here are some drugstore examples from Rite Aid to help you make sense of this phenomenon.

Rite Aid has a user-friendly rebate program where all you have to do is take your receipt home, enter a few numbers from the receipt into Rite Aid's computer system, and they send a check at the end of the month. No clipping proofs of purchase, no envelope or postage to pay, just a few clicks and the check will literally be in the mail!

Many drugstores offer products advertised as "free after rebate." Often, you can submit a rebate for the entire product value. I found the following deal just last week at the national drugstore chain Rite Aid.

> **Crest Pro Health Toothpaste $2.79**
> Submit for $2.79 rebate
> *Final Price: FREE after rebate*

Let's take it one more step to make some money. If you combine a coupon with the rebate promotion, *they'll* actually pay *you*. Here's an example:

> **Crest Pro Health Toothpaste $2.79**
> Submit for $2.79 rebate
> Use the $0.75/1 Crest coupon from 8/2 Procter & Gamble Insert
> *Final Price: FREE Plus $0.75 Profit after coupon and rebate*

Now, let's take one final step. Let's say there's an additional printable coupon worth $5 off your in-store purchase of $25 or more. This coupon may be used in addition to your manufacturer coupons and rebates. The following example has you purchase six items to reach a minimum $25 subtotal. This way, you may use the $5.00 off $25.00 coupon to make even more money. Follow along closely:

(BUY 1) Crest Pro Health Toothpaste $2.79
Submit for $2.79 rebate
Use the $.75/1 Crest coupon from 8/2 Procter & Gamble Insert
Final Price: FREE Plus $0.75 Profit after coupon and rebate

(BUY 1) ReNu MultiPlus Solution $9.99
Submit for $9.99 rebate
Use the $2.00/1 ReNu (bausch.com)
Final Price: FREE Plus $2.00 Profit after coupon and rebate

(BUY 1) Gillette Venus Razor $7.00
Submit for $5.00 rebate
Use the $2.00/1 Gillette Venus from 8/2 Procter & Gamble Insert
Final Price: FREE after coupon and Rebate

(Buy 1) Duck Brand EZ Start Frustration Free Tape 22.2 yards - $1.49
Submit for $1.49 rebate
Final Price: FREE after Rebate

(Buy 1) Werther's Original Caramel Chocolate, 5.2oz - $2.99
Submit for $2.99 rebate
Use the $0.55/1 Werthers from 4/26 Smart Source Insert
Final Price: FREE Plus $0.55 Profit after coupon and Rebate

(Buy 1) Soft White Longlife Light Bulbs 60, 75 or 100 watt 2 pack - $2.00
Submit for $2.00 rebate
Final Price: FREE after Rebate

Subtotal: $26.26
Use the $5 off $25 any store purchase printable coupon
Pay $15.96 out of pocket, plus tax
Receive one rebate in the amount of: $26.26
Final Price: Moneymaker of $10.30

See what I mean? In this deal, I still had to pay the cashier ($15.96 + tax), but at the end of the month, I'll receive a check for $26.26. That's what I call a "moneymaker."

Let's review: If you can find an item advertised "free after rebate" and you have a manufacturer coupon for $2.00 off, it becomes a $2.00 moneymaker. Drugstores often have great coupons like "$4 off a $20 purchase" or "$5 off a $25 purchase." These coupons allow you to make even more money. Rebates may allow you to make money occasionally at grocery stores, but drugstores are the primary place to find these moneymakers consistently.

The only problem with freebies and moneymakers is that these deals don't stick around for long. Even if a deal lasts all week, the products may sell out quickly if the store hasn't overstocked the items. So what's a Krazy Coupon Lady to do when she finds an empty shelf?

RAIN CHECKS

For Krazy Coupon Ladies, rain checks can be like pure gold. Picture this: A flustered Krazy Coupon Lady waits until the last day of the sale to stock up on her much needed Electrasol Dishwasher Tabs. She was out of town all week at her husband's family reunion. While camping with the in-laws in the boonies, she spent the entire time thinking about all the sales she was missing. Fun, right? When she gets home, before she showers or starts a load of laundry, she races to the store to stock up on her dishwasher tabs. She walks straight to the aisle with cleaners and detergent and sees a shelf full of...(begin the ominous music)...empty space. You guessed it. Our dear Krazy Coupon Lady waited too long and is now faced with two choices: start fuming at all the other couponers who "cleared the shelf," or take matters into her own hands by asking for a rain check.

What is a rain check?

When a sale item is out of stock, a rain check is a slip of paper that entitles you to come back later and buy at the sale price after the item is re-stocked, even once the sale period is over. Ask your store's customer service desk whether they write rain checks. Rain check policies vary by store, so make sure you check each store's rules carefully. Some stores have an expiration date on the rain check, while others don't. You will also find that some stores will have a maximum number of items for which they will give you a rain check. Typically, if the sale price involved a limit of, say, four per customer, the rain check will be limited to four as well.

Rain check tips:

- If you plan to use coupons with your rain check price, make sure that the coupons won't expire before the store gets the items back in stock. No use going through the trouble of getting a rain check just to have expired coupons defeat the purpose.

- Don't bother getting a rain check for something that is also included in a promotion (such as, "Spend $10, save $4 instantly"). Rain checks are only valid for the sale price. The store cannot honor a promo once it's over, even with a rain check.

- You cannot get a rain check on clearance prices.

- When redeeming your rain check, be courteous. Let the checker know that you'll be using one before he or she starts to ring you up. Often, checkers manually need to enter the amount, so they'll love you if they don't have to go back at the end of the transaction to void and re-enter the correct amount.

Remember, if you find a product out-of-stock, take the opportunity to ask for a rain check. (A slip of paper that allows you to come back and purchase an item for the sale price when the store has it back in stock.) If you want to stockpile the item, ask the person writing the rain check to write it up for the maximum quantity allowed. Then hurry your sweet little self over to eBay and buy all the coupons you need and head back to the store when the item is re-stocked. Easy as free rain check pie.

FAQs:

If my store doubles coupons up to $2.00 and I use a $2.50 off coupon, will the store take an additional $2.00 off? For a total of $4.50 off?

No! When the store states it will double coupons up to $2.00 in value, any coupon $2.01 or higher will receive no special treatment of any kind.

Are rebates worth the time?

Absolutely! Most rebates take less than three minutes. The first thing I do when I walk in the door from shopping with rebate items is head straight to the computer with my receipt, enter in a few short numbers, and the rebate is calculated for me. I receive my rebates in the mail once a month. Basically, I get a paycheck in the mail for shopping.

Do I have to submit UPC barcodes with all my rebates?

No. Many rebates only require you to enter a few key facts from your receipt. No bar code clipping, no stamp, no hassle. Some old-school rebates still require you to clip a UPC and mail it in.

Do you ever *really* get paid to shop?

Some grocery stores will pay overage, meaning if you have a $1.00 coupon to use on an $0.80 item, they will physically pay you $0.20 to buy the product. Most stores hold the policy to adjust the price of the coupon down to match that of the item, meaning they won't pay you money. Most KCLs will tell you that it feels like you're getting paid when you constantly get stuff for free or almost free.

If chocolate chips are on sale for $0.98 per bag and the store is out of stock, may I get a rain check for twenty bags and go ahead and pay now? My coupons expire tomorrow, so I can't wait for the re-stock, but I can pay now and then pick up the chocolate chips when they arrive, right?

Wrong! Unfortunately, you cannot prepay for items with coupons. It technically constitutes—*horrified gasp*—coupon fraud. You may get a rain check for as many items as the store allows, but you may not buy the items with a coupon until they are physically in your cart.

SECTION TWO

Taking the Reins!

CHAPTER EIGHT

Leading Your Family:

LIFE AS THE CFO

KRAZY COUPON LADY QUIZ:
WHAT KIND OF SHOPPER ARE YOU?

1. You're shopping with your young and wiggly child in the cart. As you watch your items ring through on the screen, you notice that a sale item, marked down to $1.99 rings up at regular price $2.69. What do you do?

A. Nothing, $0.69 cents is not worth the time and headache to wait for the cashier to correct the problem.

B. What screen? You've got way too much going on even to think about checking the computer screen!

C. You mention that you think the item was on sale. The checker asks, "Well, do you want me to call someone to go do a price check?" You say, "No, it's fine."

D. You tell the cashier that the item did not ring up correctly. When the cashier offers to go get a price check, you accept and thank him or her for fixing the error.

2. At the checkout, your cashier takes one look at your stack of coupons and informs you that the coupons state "one per purchase" and declines your request to use more than one, unless you're wanting to do twenty-plus separate transactions.

A. You remain calm and start explaining nicely that "one coupon per purchase" means "one per item." All it's really saying is that you can't use two $1.00 off coupons for one $2.00 product. The cashier gets mad and calls over a manager, but you politely stick to your guns. You invite them to call their own 800 guest services number to clarify, and you wait for fifteen minutes while they sort out the debacle.

B. You throw up your hands and cuss like a sailor, shouting, "I can't believe you don't know your own policies! Re-shelve these items or stick them [bleeeeeeep]."

C. You tell them you'll do separate transactions and proceed to swipe your credit card over twenty times.

D. You buy all your twenty-plus items at full price and only use one of your coupons.

3. Which of these statements best describes your attitude regarding the way stores treat those who shop with coupons.

A. "Thanks anyway!" Even if the store refuses some of my valid coupons, I'm still grateful for the ones they did accept.

B. The store should go out of its way to help me. They should open up a new checkout lane for me, and take ALL my coupons even if they don't scan, look questionable, or exceed any store limits. After all, look how much stuff I'm buying! I'm talking so much about my new obsession it's free advertising for the store.

C. My valid coupons are my currency. They are just as good as cash, and the store will treat me with respect.

D. It's okay for the cashiers and managers to huff and puff and treat me like a subclass shopper. After all, I'm slow at checkout, and I'm sure coupons are a pain.

4. You're buying an item with one store coupon and one manufacturer coupon. The item is $2.00. You're using a $1.00 off manufacturer coupon and a $0.50 store coupon. The cashier tells you, "One coupon per item, lady. You can't use both of these. Pick one." What do you do?

A. You say, "Well, I know your policy says I can use both coupons, and I'm not leaving until you ring these both through." Ask for her name and how long she's been working here. Write down all this info as if you're turning her in to the authorities.

B. You politely whip out the store's coupon policy from your binder, and show her where it states you are allowed to use one store and one manufacturer coupon together. Then, apologize to the line of people behind you. Let them know they might want to...."Pick another checkout lane, honey."

C. You take one look at that long line behind you and tell the cashier you'll just use the $1.00 off coupon and save the $0.50 for later.

D. You don't explain anything. Just turn on your pouty face and ask whether she'll please make an exception, just this once.

5. You're buying some trial size items with coupons. The items are $0.97 and your coupons are for $1.00 off, so you're gonna get them free. But guess what? Trouble at checkout! The cashier says he cannot accept a coupon that exceeds the item's value, AND coupons can't be used on trial size. What do you do?

A. You ask him to read the coupon and tell you where it says "excludes trial size" (it doesn't, you already checked), but he maintains his stance, and you storm out with no purchases.

B. You tell him his store policy states that he should simply adjust the price down to match the value of the item, so instead of taking off a full dollar, just take off $0.97 cents.

C. You insist that he must take off a full dollar because, after all, the store is going to be reimbursed for the full $1.00. Why are they stealing your $0.03??

D. You buy the trial size items anyway, without the coupons.

Now, find the answers you chose below and give yourself the corresponding points.

For example, in question 1, if your answer was "c," give yourself 3 points. Then total your score.

1) a.2 b.1 c.3 d.4

2) a.4 b.2 c.3 d.1

3) a.1 b.1 c.4 d.1

4) a.3 b.4 c.1 d.2

5) a.3 b.4 c.2 d.1

16 points +

You are well on your way to being a savvy and successful couponer! You're not afraid to stand up for fairness and policy, even if it inconveniences you to do so. You stay calm and collected and are always a picture of politeness, but you are unwavering in your dedication to getting what is rightfully yours.

7-15 points

You are still a coupon rookie! You're learning as you go, and by the end of this book, you'll be ready to assert yourself. You might be intimidated by the idea of having to go toe-to-toe with some overconfident store manager who thinks he's the king of the world. You might think you're too busy, and you don't have time to deal with shenanigans at the store. I've still got some convincing to do with you, but you'll get the hang of this soon.

Under 7 points

Stand up for yourself, girl! You deserve better than what you are accepting. Don't let others walk all over you. It doesn't make you ungrateful or rude when you calmly and assertively make sure you're treated with respect. Go look in the mirror and tell yourself that you deserve respect...and while you're there, remind yourself that you're beautiful.

Now that you know what kind of shopper you are, let's talk about the kind of shopper you can become! It's really quite simple. Treat yourself with the same honesty and respect you give others every day. Stop selling yourself short, eating the heels of your bread, and letting others walk all over you! Here's one more quiz question for you:

Imagine you just got home from one of the aforementioned coupon trips. Exhausted, you drop your grocery bags to the floor and toss your purse on the counter, only to see a shiny wrapper peeking out of the top. You walk over and find a bag of candy in your purse, a contraband candy bag thrown into your purse by your four-year-old while you were neck deep in your coupon debacle for what seemed like an eternity. Your child walks up behind you and says, "My candy! Can I have it, Mom?" What do you do?

I don't have to give you options because I already know what you're going to do. I know what kind of stand up individual you are and that you're going to take advantage of this teaching moment. Whether you're loading that four-year-old back in the car right this instant (or maybe some of us less-than-perfect folks would wait until the next day), you're going to drive him back to the store with that candy bag. I know you're going to march straight up to customer service with his trembling, sweaty little fist in your hand. I know you're going to ask him to give that candy back to the store because, "We didn't pay for it." Why are you going to all this trouble? Is it because the store might go bankrupt if it loses that $0.33 you owe it for some candy? Of course not. It's for the principle. You're teaching your child to treat others with the utmost honesty. This will likely be the last time you find surprise candy in your purse as you've just effectively taught an important parenting lesson.

It's an equally important lesson to teach this same child that, just as you should treat the grocery store with honesty and respect, the grocery store should treat you the same way. When my child watches me politely interject as my item rings up the wrong price, when my child sees me calmly and confidently speak to a store manager, I am proud of what I'm teaching. I'm glad to be raising children who know how to speak up for themselves politely.

One reader, Richelle, wrote in to tell us why she coupons. She said:

> ...I do it for lots of reasons. One, I'm addicted and I figure if I'm going to be addicted to something, why not have it be saving money? Two, because it's my way of helping out the budget. I'm fortunate enough to be able to stay home and so anyway I can help, especially if I can have fun doing it, I'm willing to try. Three, I want my kids to learn to save and be frugal too, and if you want something it's okay to wait until it's on sale so you don't have to spend all your money on it. I loved it the other night when my son said he wanted to buy something and asked whether I'd watch for a coupon so he could get it!! And last, I just love it!

We've got to stop giving our power away by being mindless consumers. I love to shop. There's something about acquiring things that gives my spirit a boost. Do you feel that way? One of the best things about couponing is that grocery shopping is no longer a mindless chore. It's a shopping trip. I satisfy my shopping urges by trolling the grocery aisles for freebies!

Another reader, Fernelius, wrote in:

> It's better to surf the Internet looking for ways to save more money than to spend the money. I once was addicted to eBay, but now I am in for the couponing and the free items. I average about $45.00 a week in savings that I normally just threw away when I would go shopping. We put that money in a jar, and it goes in the family trip fund. I like that I am teaching my kids to be frugal and really weigh the options in buying things rather than buying just to do it.

Pick another Checkout Lane, Honey isn't just about saving a few hundred bucks a month. It's about an attitude shift. It's about achieving new balance. Couponing is not a housewife's chore. It truly will become your hobby, your obsession, and what better pastime can you have than saving money? You're setting your life on track for huge success and happiness!

Lizzy writes in:

> My husband had to build me a pantry....which is now overflowing. I feel POW-

ERFUL!! Diapers used to be painful to buy....now I get them sooooo cheap.
I used to use a dull razor until it was practically rusted out. Now I get pretty
green & pink ones for practically free.

No more dull razors! I don't know which my husband likes best: having deluxe breakfast cereals stacked to our garage ceiling or saying goodbye to my prickly legs. My family enjoys name brand products, and when the ketchup bottle starts spitting, I don't spend the next twenty-four hours precariously balancing it upside down, trying to squeeze out every last drop! I just grab another full bottle from the garage. No more digging out the last bit of chapstick or cramping my fingers fighting an empty toothpaste tube. This is embarrassing, but there was a time when if my son threw a toothbrush in the toilet water, I considered soaking it in rubbing alcohol instead of tossing it. How gross is that? Now we have fresh toothbrushes when we need them. When we host guests who have forgotten something, I feel like a concierge at their service with a full menu of complimentary toiletries.

You might be a Krazy Coupon Lady if. . .
your friends find excuses to come visit
you just for the complimentary toiletries.

WE SHOULD COME HERE MORE OFTEN.

Saving $500 per month or walking out of the store with a cartload of groceries for under twenty bucks doesn't come free. You know you'll have to reallocate your time in order to make that extra hour or two per week to become a coupon shopper. Is it worth it? Of course. If you're not convinced yet, just ask yourself: who would you rather pay—the store or yourself? As the chief financial officer of my household, I know the answer. I'll pay myself every time! A few hours of my time for hundreds in my pocket. It's hard evidence to refute.

The Krazy Coupon Lady lifestyle is for *everyone*. It's for stay-at-home-moms, full-time working moms, savvy shopping dads, college students, bachelors, retired grandmas and grandpas—you name it! Although bachelors, beware. Walking around a grocery store with a cartload of groceries and your coupon binder might make you the hottest chick-magnet ever!

FAQs:

What if I don't feel comfortable standing up for myself at checkout?

You'll get there. Remember that standing up for yourself doesn't mean being rude or causing a scene. You can stand up for yourself firmly and kindly, and then everybody wins. Anyone can stand up for him or herself! I have a friend who is extremely shy and soft-spoken. When she told me she wanted to learn to become a Krazy Coupon Lady, I was concerned. I thought there was no way she would ever be able to talk back to a store manager. She has totally surprised me. She has grown in confidence like krazy! She uses the store policies to do a lot of the talking for her, but she asserts herself as well. Even if you're painfully shy or afraid to ruffle any feathers, isn't that something you'd like to overcome? I think anyone can grow into the role of becoming a sassy coupon lady.

What if the store manager is insistent, and you can't agree?

Walk away. Sometimes store managers are pretty bull-headed. Even after you show them the policy, don't be surprised if you hear lines like, "We just had a meeting addressing this," or "Well, the new policy states..." I think we often intimidate managers and they scramble for a reason to be right. In their store, they win, so after we've done our best, sometimes we have to walk away. Do so politely. Let them know, "I'm sorry, I won't be able to complete my purchase today." Then get in the car, and after you pull out of the parking lot, commence screaming. When you get home, call the corporate offices. They will invariably apologize and take care of you. Sometimes they'll even call and speak to the store manager while you're still on the line.

Shouldn't we be more understanding of a store that doesn't like coupons? Doesn't it lose money?

No! Stores are reimbursed for every penny. You aren't costing them anything, and they benefit by selling more stuff. My coupons are my currency! They are just as valid as a dollar bill. All the store has to do is mail them off to a clearinghouse that does all the sorting for them. In addition to reimbursement for the coupon's value, the store also receives up to $0.08 in handling fees per coupon, which covers the cost of this process.

The store pays a fee every time I swipe my credit card. It earns money when I pay with coupons and change. Never feel like a sub-class shopper, and never allow yourself to be treated like one.

CHAPTER NINE

Befriending the Bigwigs:
LEARNING STORE POLICIES AND
TALKING TO STORE MANAGERS

Now that you know how to clip, file, shop, talk the talk, and walk the walk, you're almost there, but you're not done yet! All your confident and sassy coupons skills are useless without a solid understanding of store policies. *Pick Another Checkout Lane, Honey* is the only book where you will find actual store policies for real U.S. stores! Each store sets its own coupon policy, and policies vary even within stores of the same chain. Find your stores and view those policies in Chapter 15.

Chances are you'll want to shop at stores besides the ones we have listed for you. For this reason, and because store policies are constantly changing, you need to know how to get a hard copy of your own store's policy.

In this chapter, you'll learn how to find a store's policy, but even after you get a copy, you'll want to speak to local store management. Take the policy into your local store manager to verify that the policy is accurate and will be enforced as it is written. Does that sound like a pain? Well, short-term, yes, long-term, no. As frustrating as it sounds, the truth is that many stores have a great policy that is unlearned and unenforced at the local level. Cover your bases by making sure you and your local stores are on the same page.

Store policies, beginner tips, and basic 101 tutorials are all offered FREE as always on TheKrazyCouponLady.com. For all the latest detailed store policy info, head on over and find your store. You will also find information on special store promotions, and all the basics in addition to current coupon deals, where we match store sales with coupons and promos for the maximum savings. You're welcome.

To search on your own for a store's policy, first try the store's official website. Use the search bar and keyword search for "coupon policy." The policies are difficult to find, so the surest way to get a copy of the policy is to email customer service under the store's "contact info" or "contact us" links. Take twenty minutes or less one afternoon, and do this for all the stores in your area where you wish to use coupons. It will be time well spent. Here's a short sample email you can send to request a copy of the policy and to make sure you're asking all the right questions.

You can find a copy of this draft email at our website. Just copy, paste it, and send it to any stores you wish!

To whom it may concern at _____,

My name is _____.

I'm learning how to become a Krazy Coupon Lady, and I'm looking forward to shopping in your store with coupons. Before I begin, I would like to request a copy of your coupon policy. Can you please clarify your policy and answer these questions?

- What kinds of coupons do you accept?
  manufacturer coupons, printable coupons, eCoupons on my preferred card?

- Do you offer store coupons? Where may I find them?

- May I use a store coupon and a manufacturer coupon on one item?

- Do you exclude any coupons? Ex: above $5 off, BOGO offers, coupons for free products?

- Do you accept printable coupons? May I print them in black and white?

- Do you match competitor prices or take competitor coupons?

- What is your policy on overage (when the value of the coupon exceeds the value of the product)?

- If the coupon exceeds the item's value, do you adjust the price of the coupon down? Ex: $1.00 off coupon on $0.97 cent product.

- Do you limit the number of coupons I may use per transaction?

- Do your employees understand "one coupon per purchase=one coupon per item," not "one coupon per transaction"?

- Does your store ever double or triple coupons?

- Concerning buy one get one offers: if your store runs a BOGO FREE promo, may I use two manufacturer coupons for the two products? Or may I only use one?

- Are individual stores allowed to impose their own rules or vary from this policy?

Thank you for taking the time to educate me on your store policies. Please mail your response to: {provide your name and address}

Sincerely,

_____

I suggest requesting the response be mailed to you if you can (rather than emailed) because a hard copy is much more powerful to have on hand. The policy will come on company letterhead, and it will have YOUR name on it. If you have a miscommunication with a local store manager, you can show your personalized, official letter from the manager's boss. This will be a powerful tool to use, and it will come in handy more times than you may know! Trust me, it's a wonderful feeling.

Even though you might feel bulletproof now, you've got one more step to take in this process.

* *

MEET WITH STORE MANAGEMENT

"But do I have to? May I please skip this step?" Sure, you can skip it if you'd like, but you may end up regretting it. One way or another, you are going to meet your store managers, I can promise you that. They'll be coming around your checkout lanes to answer checker's questions and do overrides all the time. So, you have the option either to take the initiative to make an appointment or wait for them to come talk to you. It is much easier (and wiser) to go ahead with a meeting when it's on your own terms, NOT when you're standing at checkout with a screaming toddler. After you set a meeting with the managers, they will love you! You want these managers on your side. Having a good relationship with store managers takes any stress right out of couponing.

Depending on how serious you want to get with this, there are two options.

First, if you want to go big, then call your store and ask for the general manager. When you get her or him on the phone, say, "Is there a time I can come into the store and meet with you briefly to discuss your coupon policy?" I have yet to have a manager turn me down on this request.

The second option is to go into the store, preferably during off-peak hours, and ask to speak with the manager on duty, sometimes called the "front-end manager." Whichever manager you meet with, you'll want to show up on time and take your copy of the store's coupon policy with you. Allow the manager to look over the policy and ask whether he or she is aware of all of these regulations. If you live in an area that has not yet seen the rise in Krazy Coupon Ladies, you will very likely be providing an education to the store manager, blazing a trail for all the coupon ladies and gentlemen to follow. Keep your meeting to around five minutes, ten minutes at most. The manager

You might be a Krazy Coupon Lady if...
you go a bit "Nancy Drew"
when you meet with store managers.

is certainly busy, and you want to stay on his or her good side. Make sure you cover all of these questions:

- Would you like to photocopy this policy to post or share with employees?

- Will your store enforce the policy as outlined from corporate customer service?

- What should I do in the event that a store employee or manager refuses to uphold this policy?

- Is there a number where you may be reached for such an occasion?

- Will you please write or sign your name (and possibly a cell phone number) at the bottom of this policy so I can remember that we have spoken?

Thank them profusely for their time. It is imperative that you leave a good impression with management. Make sure they know you are a valuable customer and they want your business. Assure them by your actions that you are a confident and responsible shopper. You're making every effort to learn and play by all the rules. (And now that you know the rules, GAME ON! Those in your path better step back and watch with their jaws gaping open as you work those store sales to your advantage). Maybe if they're nice enough to you, someday you'll tell them how to save all that money!!

* *

CARRY YOUR STORE POLICIES IN YOUR BINDER

Can you see how good it will feel and how powerful you will become when you have your accurate store policy and you've discussed it with the store manager? You are just about ready to start your engines and begin slashing your budget and taking names. The last thing I want to address regarding store policies is what to do with all those policies now that you've collected them and discussed them with local management.

Those boy scouts have it right: be prepared. Print each store policy and tuck it safely away in your binder, where it's out of the way but easily accessible. You will find that when a checker hasn't been educated about store policy, and the coupon beeps, requiring a response from the checker, she'll just say, "Sorry! We can't take this!" The checker will just assume the coupon is rejected. But if you have your coupon policy on hand, it's easy to nicely and firmly explain how the store's policy works.

Here's an example. You go to Target to buy one trial sized bar of soap priced at $0.97. You have your $1 off coupon (which states $1 off any sized soap). You hand the checker your item, then the coupon, and when she scans the coupon, it beeps, requiring the checker to respond. She hands the coupon back to you and says, "The system won't allow me to take this coupon." You pull out your Target Policy and say: "Your corporate policy states that you are able to adjust the coupon down to equal the amount of the item. Would you like to see a copy of your policy?"

This will generally clear up any confusion, and you and your free soap can head home to organize your shiny, towering stockpile.

• •

PROVIDE FEEDBACK

How can stores improve their written policies as well as their implementation? Through all of our feedback, of course. *Always give feedback.* If you have a poor experience with a policy or store employee, don't be too afraid or lazy to take it up with the corporate store offices. We can't expect stores to improve if we don't report the problems.

On the other side, make sure you provide just as much positive feedback as you do negative. If you have a favorite store location, one that is particularly coupon-friendly or especially helpful, please send positive feedback to corporate headquarters. If you have a favorite, knowledgeable checker, make sure you tell his or her manager how impressed you are.

I used to have a favorite grocery store, not a half-mile from my home. It had the best stock, the nicest checkers, and the most knowledgeable management. This store even clipped coupons and handed them out to customers for free! One of the store managers' names was Bill. His store was so well known as the hot coupon spot, that when I ran into policy problems at other locations, I'd say, "At my location, I was able to use both a manufacturer and a store coupon on one item…" The response would always be something like "Oh, they're too liberal with their coupon policy over at your location." Instead of complaining about the bad store, I decided to praise the one that was doing so well. I wrote a short article on TheKrazyCouponLady.com titled "Marry me, Bill." I said how awesome his store was and how much I appreciated him. It made him feel good, and rumor has it that he printed the article and put it up at his store for all the employees to see.

Remember to give feedback! Both positive and negative feedback can shape the future of these stores and their coupon policies. Communicate with stores and help them become better for all of us.

• •

Learn the Rules so You Can Play By the Rules

Learning the ins and outs of your store policy allows you to do two things. First, it allows you to play by the rules because you know the rules. What do I mean? Well, you won't have to be nervous that you're accidentally or unknowingly being unethical about something because you've taken the time to educate yourself and learn the facts. In the olden days, when I began couponing, I made many errors out of ignorance. Sure, I made these mistakes without meaning to, but I accepted responsibility for my lack of education.

I recently moved to California (so recently that I'm still driving with out-of-state plates). A co-worker mentioned to my husband, "Make sure you don't talk on your cell phone while driving. It is now illegal in California." The other day, while driving (and wishing I could pick up my phone and make some calls!), I wondered, "Between my out of state plates and my pasty white complexion, I clearly appear to be an out-of-stater. Do I have to abide by the same law as California residents?" If it weren't for my husband's co-worker, I wouldn't even know that there was this "new cell phone law." For a minute, I began to justify my actions. I said to myself, "If I were pulled over, the cop couldn't expect that I know this new law. I'm an out-of-towner!" But then I realized: if I want to drive on California roads, it is my responsibility to learn California laws and abide by them—or pay the price. The same holds true for learning store policies. Don't get by with ignorance. We all have a responsibility to learn and follow the rules.

The second thing learning the rules allows you to do is to save big. Learn the rules, because that knowledge will allow you to take advantage of things you may have once considered loopholes, but, after further inspection, you've found to be perfectly honest and legitimate ways to save big bucks!

Learn that when a store says 10/$10, it almost never means you have to buy ten to get that price. Learn that if body wash is $4.00 with an in-store "Buy one, get one free" promo, and you have two manufacturer coupons for $2.00 off, you can use BOTH of them and get the two products for free. Every Krazy Coupon Lady knows that knowledge is power. Ignorance will lead you to mistakes, either in the form of embarrassment or less-than-spectacular savings. Neither alternative is acceptable, and neither is conducive to the Krazy Coupon Lady's mantra. So seize the day, take the reins, and get out and learn your policies!

FAQs:

Do store policies change frequently?

A store may change its policy at any time. For the latest policy information, stay up-to-date at TheKrazyCouponLady.com

The Krazy Coupon Lady doesn't cover all the stores in my area. How can I find coupon match-ups for one of my local stores?

Send KCL an email, and let us know what store you wish we covered. We'll let you know whether we're planning to cover that store or refer you to someone else who does. There are many great and free coupon sites scattered across the country. Search the web to find one that covers the store where you shop.

What if I find my store is inconsistent in enforcing its coupon policy? Sometimes I can get certain deals, and other times I cannot. What do I do?

Inconsistent policy enforcement is both common and frustrating. One particular supercenter is the worst offender. The best way to combat inconsistency is to find an opportunity to talk to the head manager at your store. After your meeting, you should have the 411, and you can throw the head manager's name around the next time you have a run in with an on-duty assistant manager.

CHAPTER TEN

Playing Fair:
WHAT YOU SHOULD
KNOW ABOUT COUPON FRAUD

You know that old saying about how one bad apple spoils the bunch? It's truer than ever when it comes to couponing. Almost every Krazy Coupon Lady (including me!) can tell you a story of a mistake she made before she knew better. You're already a step ahead! After reading this book, you're going to be ten times more informed than I ever was as a coupon virgin. Why all the admonitions not to misuse the information we're giving you in this book? Why devote an entire chapter to placing my hand on my hip, tapping my foot, and shaking my finger at you? Coupon fraud is a serious and unfortunately all-too-common offense. There are a few different ways to commit coupon fraud. Some are intentional and many are unintentional.

The information in this chapter isn't anything you won't find by doing a few Google searches, but it is information that has the potential to be misused. If I were trying to give you tips on how to commit fraud, I could title this section "Become a Dirtbag 101," but I obviously don't encourage people to break the law. Remember, knowledge is power. Krazy Coupon Ladies need to be knowledgeable about what to do and what not to do.

BARCODE DECODING

Decoders are shoppers who sneak legitimate coupons past their cashiers when using them for products for which the coupon is obviously not intended. Barcode decoders try to circumvent the computerized cash registers. Decoders find coupons that will scan in and "trick" the computer into accepting the discount for the wrong product. A common example: taking a high value coupon that says it's for whitening strips and trying to use it to buy the same brand's toothpaste for free or even for overage (profit). This is completely dishonest and constitutes stealing from the store. The Krazy Coupon Lady's inbox has seen many emails advocating that decoding is a perfectly legitimate way to coupon. We have readers send in deals or freebies they obtained by misusing coupons and "sneaking" them past their checkers. These folks aren't bad people—far from it. They just don't understand what is and is not allowed in the world of coupons. *Legal and legitimate couponing means abiding by the fine print on the coupons.*

I remember the first time I heard about decoding. I was shopping with a few friends at the local supercenter, and one girl, whom I had just met, came up and showed me that as long as certain digits on the coupon match those on a product, it was okay to use the coupon. I naively believed her, and I used some coupons meant for one product on a slightly different product. Later as I did my own research at home, I quickly learned that my behavior was wrong and should never be repeated. If our checkers that night had been more thorough, they would not have allowed us to misuse those coupons, and I would have learned my lesson right then and there! Don't blindly accept advice from people who profess to know a lot about coupons without looking into and verifying the validity of what they say.

Think of the line at airport security. Is it slow? Yes. Similarly, is the meticulous scrutiny of your coupons an inconvenience? Yes. Is there profiling going on? Maybe…Cashiers are becoming more vigilant about reading the fine print on a coupon, and all of the honest couponers have to be patient as they do this. They are (understandably) trying to protect their stores from losing money. I used to get easily irritated at a cashier who felt over-entitled to scan my coupons with her eyes, close her lane, turn on her blinking light, and ask for a manager to come pat me down and read me my rights. (Okay, so they never patted me down—what would they be looking for, anyway? What does an accused fraudulent couponmaker carry on her person? A printing press?) Now I am grateful for thorough cashiers. Just like when a store clerk asks for ID when I pay by credit card for my own protection, I thank the checkers who are thoroughly examining my coupons.

On a recent shopping trip, when I handed the checker my stack of coupons, she exhaled a big annoyed breath and started to read the coupons over. She informed me she'd have to call over a manager to do an override (because of the number of coupons I was using). I had expected nothing less; this particular store always requires a management override. I thanked her for taking the extra time to make sure my coupons were valid, and I told her how grateful I was that her store recently began accepting printable coupons after a few years of denying them due to an outbreak of fraud. I went on to explain that cashiers like her would make it possible for coupon moms like me to continue to use coupons. Words can't describe the look she then gave me. She rolled her eyes and looked perfectly perturbed. At that moment, the manager walked up, and after my coupons were all cleared, I left without pressing the issue, but it makes me laugh to think about her reaction. She must have been so accustomed to shoppers being annoyed by the slow and excruciating examination process that she made me out to be the worst of all. She thought I was feeding her a bunch of sarcasm, when I was trying to pay a genuine compliment. Meticulous employees getting out their figurative magnifying glass to check each coupon ensures that their stores will not lose money on the coupons we use.

I cannot control how others interpret my words or actions. I can only make certain I act with the right intent. I always try to say, "Thank you" to a cashier who is particularly thorough. The more meticulous the cashier, the fewer fraudulent mis-uses will get past them. If stores are getting scammed, they'll be less likely to accept coupons in the future, and then everyone will lose. If your cashier doesn't look at your coupons, she's not looking at anyone else's either. Let's make it clear that we want store employees to be reading all the fine print.

• •

Expired Coupons

You cannot use a coupon after its expiration date. There are a few stores left that accept expired coupons, but you can bet your local store isn't one of them. Military members shopping at overseas commissaries may use expired coupons for up to six months past their expiration date. Visit TheKrazyCouponLady.com and find out how to send in your expired coupons each month to be distributed between one of our many adopted bases.

• •

Fraudulent Coupons

Fear of counterfeit has sometimes caused stores to stop accepting printable coupons altogether. Security measures are increasing, and scannable bar codes are reducing fraud. There has been such a huge consumer demand for retailers who will accept these printable coupons that nearly all stores accept them now. Even though most stores accept printable coupons, it's important to understand why stores may still be wary to do so.

The Coupon Information Corporation, a non-profit organization made up of manufacturers fighting coupon fraud, says:

> *Counterfeit coupons have cost manufacturers millions of dollars and have created numerous costs and challenges for retailers and other industry participants. These counterfeits have ranged from amateurish home-made ones to high quality, professional examples virtually identical to those printed by the industry. Unfortunately, even the amateurish coupons are often accepted for redemption,*

creating liabilities for a variety of industry participants. Once a counterfeit is accepted, someone, whether it is a manufacturer or a retailer, is going to have to pay for it, creating uncontrollable liabilities and unnecessary trade relations issues. Counterfeiters have forced retailers to be more aggressive in reviewing coupons at the checkout lane. The increase in front end security procedures has created consumer discomfort, increased costs, and longer lines.

Yikes. It really *does* sound like airport security when the CIC talks about it! Understanding the reason for the increasingly slow checkout and the longer lines can help us be more patient. There will always be criminals exploiting opportunities to make a buck, so get used to the skepticism and security on coupons.

The most well known way to commit coupon fraud, and the best coupon-induced way to get thrown in the clink, is to create your own fraudulent coupons. Come on now, any takers? Are you good on photoshop or paint? Is this sounding appealing to anyone? I highly doubt any of us are considering entering into the crime ring of creating fraudulent coupons.

You might be a little too krazy if... you thought making or selling your homemade coupons was a good idea.

Selling counterfeit coupons is a serious crime, punishable by fines and jail time. The problem with coupon fraud for the rest of us isn't about creating them; it's about accidentally purchasing or redeeming them. We need to learn how to spot an illegitimate coupon before we ever think about using it! Fraudulent coupons are almost always printable coupons, which is why some stores still don't accept these printables or do so with much hesitation.

REMEMBER THE RED FLAGS

Things that might make your cashier question the validity of your printable coupons:

- Expiration Date: Your cashier may check for unusually long expiration periods or dates that appear to have been altered. Valid printable coupons often have short expiration periods, usually 30-90 days.

- Easily Scannable Barcode: Proper printable coupons use technology that creates clear barcodes. Your cashier will look for barcodes that are unusually fuzzy or appear to have been altered.

- Legal Language: Manufacturers include legal language to protect against fraud and/or misredemption. Words such as "coupons are not to be altered, copied, transferred, purchased, sold, etc." are included on most printable coupons.

- Instructions for the retailer: Your cashier may look for mailing address and directions.

- Multiple Coupon Prints: Your cashier may look for multiple prints (more than two) of the exact same coupon. Most valid printable coupons provide print controls that limit customers to one or two prints of the same coupon.

The Krazy Coupon Lady doesn't endorse buying printable coupons online. If you do find a printable coupon for sale on eBay, make sure you can also print it from your computer and that it is from an obviously legitimate website. Most manufacturers print something like "Do Not Transfer" on their coupons, so buying coupons is technically illegal. In an effort to comply with this largely unenforced law, coupon sellers always sell with the following disclaimer, "You are not paying for the actual coupon. You are reimbursing me a handling fee for the time it takes me to clip and mail it to you," or something similar.

Printable coupons nearly always have a print limit—usually two prints per computer. The best way to accumulate a greater number of printable coupons is to ask family and friends to print and mail them to you. Or ask your neighbors or in-town relatives. TheKrazyCouponLady.com is another great place to ask for coupons. Our readers are constantly happy to help each other out. Just leave a comment and ask for someone to trade you some coupons. There is always someone else looking for a different coupon you could print, and before you know it, you've got a successful trade. A word of caution: remember that you give out your mailing address at your own risk. If you want to keep that private, you'll have to trade locally and meet up at a popular grocery store or public place.

Again, when your cashier is being slower than molasses and scanning each and every printable coupon as if searching for a secret treasure map watermark, have patience. A few slimeballs ruin it for everyone. Remember to think of it like airport security—a necessary inconvenience.

FAQS:

What if my cashier accuses me of photocopying my coupons?

The easiest way is to point out the individual barcode numbers in the upper right hand corner, found in many printable coupons. If you find a particular store consistently has a problem with your coupons, don't clip your coupons until you're at the checkout. This way the cashier can look at the url source and the date and time-stamp. This should help to prove your coupons are valid and not photocopied.

What if my valid coupon won't scan?

This could happen for a few reasons. First, if your printer is from the Stone Age, you may not get a clear barcode. Second, some coupons from manufacturers' sites print in a different format from the norm, and their barcodes may not always scan. You can explain to your cashier where you found your coupon and that it is valid, and the cashier should manually enter the coupon into the computer. Be aware that some stores maintain a policy to deny any coupon that does not scan.

What if my coupon has many of the "red flag" indicators of a fraudulent coupon, but I still think it's legitimate?

The best place to check the validity of a coupon is to find its source. If it comes from a manufacturer site or from a huge marketing company like coupons.com or smartsource.com, it is a legitimate coupon.

Feel free to send suspicious coupons to The Krazy Coupon Lady for verification. Printable coupons posted on KCL will have been through a rigorous verification process.

Why does KCL advocate buying coupons if the coupons clearly state "void if transferred"?

I wouldn't jump off a cliff just because everyone else was doing it, but I will buy coupons online. The manufacturer puts out a coupon to sell products, and by transferring coupons, the redemption rate has never been higher. Be very careful that you never buy fraudulent coupons. But other than that, in my expert couponing opinion, there's nothing wrong with paying someone for his or her time in clipping and mailing you coupons.

What is barcode decoding?

Coupon clipping websites are very main stream and those purchasing coupons are widespread. Barcode decoding is the practice of misusing coupons for products for which they are not intended. Decoders learn how to trick the cash register so the coupons will be accepted as long as the cashier doesn't read the wording on the coupon. Barcode decoding is dishonest, fraudulent, and illegal.

CHAPTER ELEVEN

Fight the Crazy:
HOW NOT TO GO
NUTS AT CHECKOUT

During your first few shopping trips as you use your new krazy coupon skills, you may feel a bit like you're stepping out on the high dive for the first time. When you get in line to pay, you may feel an air of uncertainty, the looming fear of something going wrong, and the impending confrontation that might ensue. But just like the high dive, standing at the top and over-analyzing is the worst part (well, that and the whole wearing a bathing suit in public thing). So take a deep breath and step in line; it'll be over soon, it's never as bad as you think it might be. And as you push your cart out the door after your first successful trip, you'll experience the couponer's "buzz", and you'll be hooked for good! So go ahead and don't be afraid to make a splash.

I've got a few more tips that are going to make certain you're totally prepared. Let's ensure that you can, in fact, swim before we tell you to jump.

Do you know what can make or break your couponing experience? How organized you are when it's time to check out. Here's how to keep your sanity:

1. Get organized before you leave the house. First, make a list of what you want to buy. You might choose to write yours by hand, or just print the store's coupon match-ups from TheKrazyCouponLady.com. If you plan to purchase items that are part of a Catalina promo where you will be doing multiple transactions, do yourself a favor and write out your list, separating each transaction. Write the item, price, and quantity you plan to buy. Have a calculator by your side and make sure to take it in your purse to the grocery store. If you're not organizing your pre-clipped coupons by category, find your coupons, and clip them now, before you leave the house. Place them in an envelope or in the front of your binder where they'll be easy to find.

2. Choose wisely the time of day that you shop. I have found that in the morning, early afternoon, or late at night is best for me. You and your checker will be less stressed if there is not a line behind you. In fact, your checker may enjoy having something to do to kill the time during a slow shift. Don't try to do five separate transactions with eighty coupons during the 5:00 p.m. rush and then act surprised when you get a grouchy checker.

3. Just for moms: If you're like me and you have young children, the key is to do your shopping early in the morning or right after naps. It's hard enough for a kid to behave at the grocery store, so I try my best not to take them out when they're already cranky and exhausted. Another note for those with kids: checking out as a Krazy Coupon Lady is going to be a much longer and more intensive process than you're used to. It's worth it, but remember that your kids will need something to do while you get your coupons rung through. You won't regret packing some toys or snacks to entertain your kids at checkout. Check your grocer's bakery to see whether they have free cookies or snacks for children and if so, make that your last stop before checkout. The ideal first shopping experience would be to shop without kids, if possible, so you can totally focus on what you're doing. The first trip or two, consider shopping late at night when your spouse is home or even getting a babysitter for your daytime shopping trip. Couponing will soon be second nature, but if you have the luxury of a babysitter close by, take her up on any offer she's made to watch your kids for an hour or two while you go shopping, just until you get the hang of it.

4. Consider shopping with a friend. Friends make everything more fun. This is especially true for beginning Krazy Coupon Ladies. On a big, multi-transaction trip, having one person to watch the items ring through and hand the cashier the coupons while the other person sets items onto the conveyor belt and separates them into transactions is an absolute lifesaver. Even on smaller trips, it's still great to shop with a buddy. You can share coupons and take turns watching each other's kids if need be or helping each other check out one at a time.

5. Talk to your cashier before your transaction begins. Greet them and let them know you're going to be using coupons with your purchase. If you're participating in a Catalina promotion, make sure to ask whether the Catalina machine is on and working! (You would not believe how often they're turned off or non-functional. Most customers don't care a bit, so the store doesn't have much reason to upkeep the machines). If you're planning to do several separate transactions, let your cashier know. Sometimes if I say, "I'm doing five different transactions with coupons today. Is this lane okay?", they'll either open a new lane for me, or they'll pull across behind me the coiled black wire that holds the "this lane closed" sign. They don't do that very often, but I love it when they do. It's nice not to have to say, "Pick another checkout lane, honey" eighteen times. If I am shopping during a time of day that is busy, I only put one transaction on the conveyor belt at a time. This way, if a line starts to form behind me, I can finish my purchase and get back in line.

Ask your cashier how she would like to take your coupons. Would she like to scan an item and then take the coupon? Or would she prefer to scan everything through and then take all my coupons? I find cashiers usually prefer the latter, but I still talk them through the stack of coupons. I'll let them know the quantity and value of each coupon as they scan them in. And I'm ready to answer any questions they might have. The easier I can make their jobs, the happier they are—and that's always a good thing! If you are particularly Type A, or if you are nervous about cashiers not ringing in some of your coupons, insist that they ring up one item, and then the coupon. This will help you keep track of your savings and will make sure each coupon gets scanned.

6. Do not be afraid to ask for a member of management to come clarify something for you. Often, you know more about the store coupon policy than the checkers, so don't be afraid to ask nicely for a manager to explain something to you. Many times, I have had them call over a manager, and it ends with the checker saying, "Huh. I never knew that!"

7. Keep a copy of the store's coupon policy in your binder. Keep the store policy with you, and don't be afraid to show it off. The reason you went through the trouble of getting a copy of the policy is twofold: first, to educate yourself, and second, to let it do your talking at the register. One reader writes:

> *Thank you for insisting that we keep the store policies with us while shopping. I just returned from a shopping trip that would have been a waste of time had I not been carrying the policy. My checker was uninformed of the store's policy, and I may have been too nervous to stand up for myself had I not had a written copy to use as reference. I was able to pull out the store's policy and have the checker read it. He immediately accepted the coupon and apologized for the trouble!!*

8. Cashier profiling: It's real, and I'm endorsing it! Once I am ready to checkout, I take a mental inventory of the available checkers. I'm a profiler. I look at the checker and decide whether he or she is going to be good. And, yes, I base this completely on stereotypes. Judge me if you must. If there are young, male checkers available, I go to them every time. Not because I'm trying to sneak anything past them, but just because I've found they are generally low maintenance. I don't have to whip out my policy or explain every word of fine print. Once you become a regular at your store, you will know whom to go to...and the good checkers will probably know you by name, and maybe they'll even have your store loyalty card phone number memorized. I'm still waiting for a love connection between a Krazy Coupon Lady and her checker.

You might be a Krazy Coupon Lady if...
your favorite cashier knows your family
by name and your preferred card by heart.

Armed with this knowledge, you're ready for success. You can go shopping with confidence and expect only the best. Expect the best, but prepare for the worst. Brace yourself, as I'm about to tell you about my worst shopping experience to date. I hope that for you, it won't get any worse than this. I was shopping at that oh-so-friendly supercenter where we've all likely shopped. I had about twenty items to purchase, each with its own coupon. Most of the items were to be totally free, and I would just be paying sales tax. The cashier was friendly enough, as most cashiers usually are. The checker scanned all my items through, bagged them, and we were almost done... or so I thought. She started scanning the coupons, and the coupons began beeping and misbehaving. I had expected this, since I was using coupons that exceeded the value of the items (e.g., the soaps were $0.99 and my coupons were for $1.00 off). I explained to the cashier how to adjust the price down, but she went ahead and called a manager over. Although it can be frustrating when checkers call managers about every little thing, remember that checkers get in trouble if they do something wrong or against the rules. They are just being careful, so Krazy Coupon Ladies should be patient with them.

The manager stormed over like the very-past-middle-age-woman-who'd-been-working-way-too-long-at-this-supercenter-and-was-mad-at-the-world she was. She took one look at my coupons and told me I couldn't use them because they all said, "One coupon per purchase." She glared at me. "You may only use one of these coupons." I explained to her that one coupon per purchase means one coupon per item, and when she didn't understand, I asked to speak to another manager. When the second manager joined her, neither one would listen to my explanation of its store's policy. I asked whether there was anyone else I could speak with so they called out the "front end manager." (How many levels of managers are there? None of which is the actual store manager. Apparently, they keep finding new ways to promote mediocrity at this establishment). He started off upset, angry that he had to bother with a customer. He agreed with the other managers, but he took it a step further and began questioning the validity of my coupons. He sneered, "How do I know these aren't fake?" These weren't even printable coupons. These were clearly from inserts, on shiny paper, the whole bit.

It gets worse. He then told me he was going to refuse me service. That's right; he told me I couldn't buy anything. He told me the store has a right to refuse service to anyone. I was upset but refused to back down. I told him he'd have hell to pay if he refused to serve me just because I was trying to shop with coupons. I then proposed, "If you think purchase means transaction (which it doesn't) then let me do twenty-plus transactions." He laughed out loud, threw up his hands and said, "Fine, do them all separately!" and walked away. Whew! I spent the next twenty minutes paying separately, and my only regret is that I should have swiped my credit card (so the store could pay a fee each time) instead of paying in cash.

Of course, I set up an appointment with the head manager at the supercenter. When I met with him, I showed him the perfectly and obviously legitimate coupons I was trying to use and asked what he was going to do to rectify this situation. Although this man was polite, he was totally clueless about coupons and about policy. He wanted to look at my binder and grill me on where customers get coupons. I had my notepad with a bunch of questions for him, and he wasn't able to answer many of them. The supercenter where I shopped is one of the worst places to coupon. Corporate has a policy, but it is officially up to each individual store to enforce its own version of the policy, and the store where I shop has an official policy to leave it up to the managers on duty. When I asked for an apology from the managers who had mistreated me, I was declined. I asked to receive an apology in writing and this is what I received a few weeks later:

> *I wanted to take this opportunity to apologize for the confusion in policy and let you know that we would love the chance to have you back in our stores.*
>
> *Signed, Curly, Mo & Larry*
> *(names have been changed to protect the*
> *three customer service-challenged employees)*

I'm not telling this story to scare you. Chances are you won't run into anything nearly as bad as that experience. The lesson is just that no matter how prepared you are, you'll sometimes still get the run around. You'll then have the choice as the consumer whether you wish to take your business elsewhere, or go back for more deals on the chance that you might get a manager who knows the policy. Looking back, I can laugh at that ridiculous day. I have since learned to keep my cool and walk away before the situation escalates. When a polite manager is simply unaware of the store policy, it's easy to explain and help him or her out. But when someone starts attacking you and treating you like a criminal, your resolve to stay polite will truly be tested.

Generally speaking, you're going to be just fine. In fact, you'll make some great friends out of the cashiers and employees at your local grocery stores. Just remember to play nice. Be courteous to your cashier, the managers, and fellow shoppers. It's okay to question what a cashier is telling you and to ask for clarification from a manager, but be polite. If you need to clear the shelf of an item, consider asking to special order. If you are going to be doing multiple transactions, shop during the slow hours and let other customers go in front of you in line. Follow the store policies and the individual coupon rules. Don't expect stores to bend their rules or make an exception for you. Respect the expiration dates, quantity limits, and manufacturer's rules. Most of the time, stores will treat you with respect when you treat their store policies with respect. Your couponing experience will go *so* much more smoothly if you prepare for your trip by making a list and grouping your coupons together. It's amazing how much nicer I am if I am not stressed about getting all my coupons together come check out time.

One last thought: conduct yourself so you wouldn't be embarrassed if you ran into an old friend or neighbor at the store. I've heard horror stories about women racing for diapers or even grabbing them out of other shoppers' baskets or hands. Don't be that shopper. They give everyone a bad name.

Do you ever get really angry in the store?

Yes. Oh, yes! And I must admit, I got worked up a time or two when I was just starting out in this whole coupon-world. Now I've learned that the best way to get what you want is to bulk up on knowledge and leave your ego at the door. Stay calm, pull out a copy of the store policy, and try to reason with and teach the cashiers and managers how their own coupon policy operates. It's baffling, but at this point in the book, you already know much more than the average cashier.

Why do you like young male cashiers? Isn't that sexist?

Well, maybe it is sexist. But I find that young male cashiers are generally more easygoing, and when I share a point of coupon policy with them, they are more likely to accept it than other cashiers. They are generally impressed by my coupon savings and want to know how I do it. Sometimes, other cashiers have been immediately skeptical, thinking this is too good to be true, and that I must be a scammer. Feel free to conduct your own case study and get back to me with the results, but if the cashier smiles at the beep of a coupon, it doesn't take Pavlov to tell me that this is the kind of cashier I'll be going back to again and again.

How long do you take at checkout?

Using coupons doubles your checkout time. After the cashier rings through all your groceries, you have reached the halfway point. Now the cashier will ring through each of your coupons. If you have complications or a manager's approval is needed, additional time is required. Don't freak out when you read this, but the longest I've spent in a checkout line is almost an hour. One of my first coupon trips, I did about ten transactions in one morning. It was a slow process but well worth it!

This is too overwhelming! How am I going to do this?

Relax! You can do it, and at this point in the book, you already have most of the knowledge you need to be successful. There are two easy tips for success. First, choose the time of day you go to the store wisely. *Don't go at rush hour.* Your trip will be much more relaxed if you shop during a slow time. Second, start small. Plan on only doing one transaction at a time on your first few trips. Make a shopping list, and calculate all your coupon savings before you leave the house. Keep your transactions small (under twelve items on your very first trip), and you'll soon be able to do more and more until you're a pro.

I don't want to argue with my checker!
Is there any way I can avoid it?

Your best shot to avoid an altercation is to carry your store policy. Let the policy do the talking if you can.

My checker is unwilling to take my coupons.
Should I still go ahead and buy the items in my cart?

No! Do not buy the items if your coupons are refused. Politely let your checker know that you will not be purchasing the items at this time. Follow up with your manager or corporate office on the phone. When the matter is resolved, go back to the store and use your coupons.

Chapter Twelve

Share the Coupon Love

Believe it or not, I'm not a salesperson. I don't even *like* salespeople, generally speaking. I cringe at multi-level marketing and would rather shred my coupon inserts (and that's *really* saying something) than pressure others into buying something for my personal gain—even though many great, legitimate businesses operate successfully with that strategy. If I'd collected all the invitations I've received to sales parties (tupperware, jewelry, books, candles, cooking supplies, you name it), many from people I hardly knew, I'd have a mountain. I've never had a knack for sales. In college I signed up to sell makeup and failed miserably. No pink Cadillac for me! I'm just not comfy as a saleswoman.

So how did I end up here, writing and selling this book? A couple of things make me, (the world's worst salesperson) want to get others involved in couponing. First, I'm so proud of the fact that other than the cost of the book, all the information you need is free. No monthly subscription fees, no donations, no nothing. The Krazy Coupon Lady might be krazy not to charge, but I'm sincerely excited about helping families like yours save money. Don't crown me with sainthood yet. TheKrazyCouponLady.com earns revenue through affiliates and advertisers, which allows the site to remain totally free for all readers. Your patronage is all the business I need.

Call me corny; call me idealistic. This information will enrich your life. Optimistic?

Maybe. But these skills, and especially the mental shift that comes along with them, is life changing. Something this valuable is not meant to be hoarded but to be shared, to be shouted! So don't think you've stumbled upon your piece of the golden pie and that you should quickly hide it so as not to share or compete for products. The information is meant to help as many homes as are willing to listen.

You might be a Krazy Coupon Lady if...
your husband offers you as a coupon tutor
to his friends & you say he's pimping you out.

Once you get krazy, the subject of couponing will come up naturally all the time. Almost every time I shop, I'm approached and asked about my binder or my cartload of twenty-four laundry detergents. I explain to these people how I do it and how they can save money, too. I then tell them about our website and ask whether they'd like to know more. I feel like a Christian missionary spreading Bible messages and inviting folks to church. Sometimes the shoppers I speak with are thrilled, and other times they think I'm nuts. One of our Kraziest Coupon Guy readers, Rick, described his experience trying to convince other people to use coupons this way:

> You would have thought I had asked them to go to a chiropractor instead of a doctor or believe in the wave theory vs. particle theory of light or the hope that Jen and Brad will ever reunite.

The skeptics will always think something about your claims is too good to be true or criminal. Don't let the skeptics bother you. Just remember that once you figure this stuff out, you can help other people achieve their financial goals, too.

Here is a story from a reader who is sharing the coupon love:

> I just started this coupon thing two weeks ago…I have a brother-in-law who has struggled with stage 4 melanoma for the last four years. He is unable to work, and his outcome is very uncertain. My sister has to be the sole breadwinner in her family. They were a young couple and had no life insurance when he was diagnosed. Often times we wanted to do more for them besides watch the kids and clean their house.
>
> This couponing allows me not only to let her know about these easy deals that she can take part in, but also to send food her way to ease some of those burdens.
>
> So thank you KCLs!!!! There are many ways you make a difference. You've given me an opportunity to help them. — Sara

Think of all the ways you can give back or help someone else by couponing. Here are just a few ideas:

- Donate to your local food bank. When you've got mac and cheese or breakfast cereal coming out your eyeballs, and it goes on sale for $0.25 again, why not spend ten bucks and donate twenty-five boxes of cereal to the foodbank? Your groceries are way more valuable than a cash donation when you can shop like that. You might even talk to your local food bank and see whether they'd like any help with their shopping.

- Donate toiletries or food to a women and children's shelter. How about all those $0.17 bottles of shampoo? How much can your family go through in a year, really? And you know that sales cycle through regularly. Wouldn't it be great if the shelter had so many toiletries they could send some full bags home when the women get back on their feet? Shelters often accept diapers, toys, games, school supplies, and many of the other items we know exactly how to get for super cheap.

- Donate to nursing homes. One of the items I frequently donate is Bayer Blood-Glucose monitors. Often Bayer releases high value coupons that make these products free. Monitors are usually about $40-50, so if I can buy ten of them and donate them, it's quite the contribution. Take your kids with you to make your donation. You'll teach them how important it is to give, and the residents will enjoy seeing them.

- Donate your expired coupons! Did you know that overseas military families can use coupons up to six months after expiration? Join with KCL in sponsoring our military base. Come on over to a website for the latest details.

There are countless ways to give back with the items you receive with coupons. Call your local hospital, Boys and Girls Club, Ronald McDonald House, or church and see what items they need. Maybe they'll name something you have stockpiled. If you don't already have the items they need, you can easily put them on your radar and watch for deals over the next month. The only thing more satisfying than stockpiling your own garage is giving away food and supplies to someone who needs it.

· ·

HELPING OTHERS HELP THEMSELVES

My favorite way to pay it forward comes from the Chinese Proverb, "Give a man a fish and you feed him for a day. Teach a man to fish and you feed him for a lifetime." I like to say, "Give a woman a basket of food and feed her family for a day. Give a woman a lesson on coupons and feed her family for a lifetime!" Teach your family and friends how to save 70% on their grocery bills. Even after just a month of couponing, you'll be ready to dole out points of wisdom and help someone else make this journey to become another one of the Krazy Coupon Ladies. Jump on an opportunity to teach a volunteer class in your community. Instead of just dropping off the toiletries at the women's shelter, ask whether you'd be welcome to teach a class on money management and share with them a few of your strategies. Teach a class for your church to the adults or even to the teenagers. Why not start young when learning to be frugal?

· ·

READY...SET...GO!

You can do this. Taking the reins is just what The Krazy Coupon Lady is all about.

I remember participating in a high ropes course as a teenager. Was it fun? Yes. Was it terrifying? Absolutely. One of the obstacles was a tiny wire ladder that took me to the top of a telephone pole. Then the task was to walk across a telephone wire with only another couple of wires to hold onto. My emotions were a frantic mix of fear and excitement. I had the desire to climb up that ladder and walk out on the wire, but it was hard to take the first step. On the other end of that wire, standing on another telephone pole, stood my coach. He encouraged me and believed in me (and reminded me of my harness that would prevent me from falling to my death). As I stood with one foot on the wire, I knew I had committed, and it was now my job to go for it. I looked down to the ground where all my girlfriends stood to encourage me. Then I realized I was being overdramatic and I walked out onto the wire. It was a rush and tons of fun, especially the zip line ride down.

Couponing is your high wire. You want to do it, and you know it's going to be fun, but it's still scary to take those first steps. TheKrazyCouponLady.com is going to be your coach. Ask your questions and soak in all the information the site has to offer. You'll be coached through until you reach the other side. I'm on the site every day (if not every hour) answering questions and guiding you through the process. Come to KCL to meet your team of girlfriends who will encourage you from down below. You won't find any judgment or name-calling on KCL. No question is too stupid, and if you make an error, we'll help you know what to do next time without jumping down your throat or calling the coupon police. We're women helping women, and we love our sprinkling of coupon guys too! If you're comfortable in a highly frugal, highly estrogenized environment, come on over.

Are you envisioning your surplus monthly budget? Can you see yourself confidently speaking to a store manager at checkout? Are you ready to re-allocate your time and make this a priority for your family? Make sure to keep track of all your savings and send The Krazy Coupon Lady a letter in a year when you reach $10,000. We'll start a club. And think of the bragging rights!

FAQs:

What if I don't feel like I have the means to donate?

Do not feel obligated to donate. Your first and most important mission is to help yourself. Build your stockpile, get out of debt, be financially independent, and take your power back. Once you have a surplus of a few items, you can consider donating. If you feel like it's too much, don't worry about donating right from the start. Take care of yourself first, and then you'll be able to help others.

What if I don't want to share my couponing secrets for fear that my stores will become overrun with couponers?

Others are going to try to figure out how to coupon. When they hear your deals or those of someone else, they will try to cash in on those same deals with or without your help. Without you, they are bound to make mistakes and break some rules unintentionally. Everyone will be better off if you help him or her learn how to do it right the first time.

SECTION THREE

Taking it to the Bank

Now that you have all the tools to save a massive amount at the grocery store, let's talk about what you're going to do with all the money you are saving. Some of you will coupon to survive, and that's just fine. For you, there is no money left in your account at the end of the month. For others, you'll start to see that your checking account has more and more wiggle room the longer you coupon. Either way, let's talk. Don't get me wrong; I'm no Dave Ramsey or Suze Orman, although I have read books from both of them. I'm no accountant or economist or other expert VIP. I am just a stay-at-home mom who has learned to live on less and can now afford the things that are important to me.

The best part about learning how to budget like a KCL? I'm not depriving you of any one thing. I'm teaching you how to get what you want at a price you can pay—not a price you can "charge".

Jean Chatzky, financial analyst for *The Today Show* writes in her book *The Difference*:

There are only four things standing in the way of any one individual and financial security.

- You have to make a decent living.

- You have to spend less than you make.

- You have to invest the money you're not spending so that it can work just as hard for you as you are working for yourself.

- You have to protect yourself and this financial life you're building so that a disaster—large or small—can't come along and take it all away from you.

These points aren't rocket science. Just like the principles in this book, they don't exactly make your eyes glaze over with their complexity. It's common sense. But it never hurts to live your financial life on tried and true common sense practices! Remember, couponing isn't about saving nickels and dimes. It is about saving enough money to make a big difference in your budget and build a stockpile to protect you in an emergency. Soon your family and your finances will be thriving with the sound implementation of these principles. That light at the end of the tunnel might seem far away for some, which is why the following section is geared toward the many of you who are already in debt, struggling to pay your bills, and becoming desperate. Don't give up; hope is not lost. Congratulations! You're about to become a coupon survivor.

You might be a Krazy Coupon Lady if...
you never undervalue your coupons. . .
even when you should.

CHAPTER THIRTEEN

Couponing to Survive

Let's start with those of you who are couponing because there is no money for groceries in your budget. Maybe your spouse is out of work. Perhaps your family is growing faster than your income or maybe you're up to your eyeballs in credit card debt. Whatever the reason, *there is hope.*

. . . .

HEATHER'S STORY:

Several years ago, my husband and I looked at our income and our expenses and realized we were in some financial trouble. We had just had our second child, and we projected that in a few months we wouldn't comfortably be able to make all our payments. So, we decided to take action and get drastic. We put our house up for sale and made an offer on another house thirty minutes away. The new house was smaller, older, and half an hour away from our friends and family (and from the shopping I loved!). We sold our house and moved our family to a little city where we knew no one. As drastic as this was, we weren't done yet. This move allowed us to lower our monthly expenses, but we also wanted to increase our monthly income. My husband found a second job, and within a few months we were able to lower our expenses by about 30% and raise our income by 30%.

If you are living paycheck to paycheck (or even worse, with the help of a plastic card), it's time to stop. Evaluate your situation and get as drastic as your situation requires.

The two basic ways to become more financially secure are (1) spend less and (2) make more. Not exactly advanced calculus, right? But like all too many things in life, these principles are a little tougher to implement than they sound.

Spend Less

If you're anything like me, you need more specific guidance than someone just saying, "Hey, spend less!" Here are a few tips to help you scale down your expenses and take control of your funds.

- -

WRITE OUT A BUDGET

Make, use, and stick to a budget. For me, that means no debit card in my wallet...seriously! I give myself envelopes with cash in them for each of my categories. When my cash is gone, I am done spending for the month. My categories include:

1. Groceries: I use a weekly budget for this category, rather than monthly.

2. Household/Miscellaneous Spending: this includes little trips to Target, McDonald's, the drycleaner, etc.

3. House Maintenance: this gets mostly used at Home Depot and usually gets spent on paint, weed killer, etc.

4. Kids: this is the envelope I bring to Chuck E. Cheese, Miniature Golfing, or the Water Park.

5. Date Night: I try to be religious about date nights. Some weeks, they are what keep me sane. We don't do anything extravagant, usually just dinner with a

coupon and a dollar movie—but having it budgeted gets us out and I need that. Even if your budget is really tight, set aside $10 per month. Find ways to do things for less. Take a walk, get ice cream, or put the kids down and rent a movie. You can even check out our website for free RedBox codes.

. . . .

Purge your pocketbook

Cut back on extras. It may sounds heartless, but as they say, a sharp knife is better than a dull spoon. Break up with whatever is holding you back. Ditch the cable TV, ditch the gym memberships, and stop eating out. You can watch all the good TV shows free online anyway, the park is a nice (free!) place for a jog, and with your couponing, you'll have plenty of groceries to work with at home. Get rid of anything you can live without.

Have a garage sale and sell big items that you haven't used for a few years on Craigslist. Sure, if it's a grandfather clock that's been in your family for three generations, you can keep it. But look around and get rid of your outgrown clothes, unused toys, and over-indulgent things you really shouldn't have bought in the first place. Be ruthless about what you get rid of. Ask yourself, honestly, "Have I used this in the last year or two?" If the answer is no, it's gotta go. I recently (and sadly) parted with some pretty hot designer jeans that I'm just not fitting back into and finally decided to sell on eBay. While it was sad to say goodbye to that small of a bottom, it was pretty nice to have an extra fifty bucks.

. . . .

Eliminate credit card debt

Before you can pay down your debt, you must get real about the debt you have. Find your credit statements, or call your credit companies. Write down on paper the num-

ber and balances of all your credit cards. When I know I'm overeating, I avoid the bathroom scale like the plague. I go months without making eye contact with it. Within these months, I can easily gain five to ten pounds. Then one morning I get brave and in my moment of resolve, run into the bathroom, step on the scale, and look at the number. It usually ruins the rest of my day, and I feel a bit depressed. But this day is always the beginning of the next phase where I buckle down and re-lose that five to ten pounds. I run through this cycle over and over. But I have never once been able to lose any weight without first stepping on the scale to weigh the damage. I can't lose weight until I have the hard numbers. Paying off debt is the same as losing weight. Without the actual numbers in front of you, you won't succeed. I know it sounds scary, but don't be afraid of totaling your credit card balances. Right now! Put this book down and go get your statements. One proven method you may use when paying off your credit card debt is to begin paying extra on the card with the lowest balance; another method is to begin by paying on the card with the highest interest rate. Once you completely pay off the first card, take the money you were paying on the first card and put it toward the next smallest card, and so on. Do whatever you need to do to become debt-free.

* *

Eliminate car payments

If you have a car payment, sell your car and buy something reliable enough to get you from point A to point B (or, in couponing, from Safeway to Walgreens). There is no use driving a Lexus while you are living paycheck to paycheck. That's like putting on your prom gown every day for dinner at McDonald's. Sell your car. Don't trade it in. Don't lease. Sell and pay cash for a car you can afford. With the money you'll be saving away with couponing, if it's that important to you, you'll get your Lexus back soon enough, and this time you'll be able to afford it!

Make More

Maybe your household has one income, or maybe you have two. You may already be working full-time or perhaps you're a stay-at-home mom. Either way, figure out a way to bring in some more cash. The rest of this chapter addresses people who are currently staying home with their children or would like to begin staying home soon, but you can adjust these principles so they work for you, whatever your situation may be.

* *

Commit

I love to start projects. I love to have a great idea, and I love the exhilaration of beginning something new. It's the finishing that always bogs me down! About halfway through a project, the glamour is gone, the work becomes a reality, and my attention span is mostly spent. This is where the real test of my spirit begins…and reveals character I'm still working to improve. If you're serious about making money, you have to be serious about seeing this vision all the way through. Don't expect to give it a try, and then, if it doesn't smell like roses in three months, dream and scheme up a new idea. Commit and stick to it!

Newsflash: all those spam emails in your inbox offering $1,000 per week by working from home are big whopping lies. If it sounds too good to be true, it is. There are no get-rich quick schemes and there are no magic diet pills (and if there were, Oprah would have already told you about them). There are two things to which I attribute my corner of success: one is God's blessings in my life and the other is LOTS of hard work. I think Jillian Michaels, trainer from *The Biggest Loser,* said it best: "I believe in blood, sweat and tears." Though she may have been referring to a workout, it really all boils down to discipline. So, do like Jillian says, "Unless you puke, faint, or die, keep going!"

. . . .

FIND YOUR PASSION

What do you enjoy? If you had to spend four hours a day doing something, what would it be? Is there any way that your hobby or some related field could earn you an income? If you scrapbook, could you sell your services or pre-packaged materials? Could you buy products wholesale and resell them online? If you love working out, could you teach classes from your home or a local park? Maybe a "Mommy and Me" class? Think about something that is really worthwhile in your life that you'd love to share with others. Teach a class, voice lessons, music lessons, do tutoring of any kind. Offer babysitting or even clean houses.

A dear friend of mine, Arlynne, mother of six children, needed to supplement her family's income during the time of her husband's unemployment. But how can a mother of six have time to work, especially with the youngest two boys too young for school? Arlynne got creative and decided to clean bathrooms or houses a few days a week with her two littlest boys in tow. Although her job is neither glamorous nor easy, she makes it work in order to supplement her family's income. She's a wife, a mother, and not afraid to roll up her sleeves and do hard work. And whether she's scrubbing a floor or strutting across it, she looks good doing it! She's got confidence, she's got sass, and she wears it well, no matter which of her many hats she's wearing. That is what being a Krazy Coupon Lady is all about.

Whatever your business vision, can you come up with a way to have zero overhead cost? If you have business expenses, get creative with financing. When I needed to print business cards for the first time, I didn't pay a printer. I found a stationery company and offered them advertising space on my website in exchange for business cards. Many of my business expenses have been financed in the same manner. I remember being a little nervous to go out and ask for swaps or get ad accounts on my website, but I didn't let that stop me, and you shouldn't either. Find your niche and then find others who are trying to appeal to the same demographic. You can swap products or advertising and build positive networking relationships at the same time.

EVALUATE TIME

Where and when will you have time for this new endeavor? What can you cut from your life to make room for this? Don't add one more giant chore to your platter. You'll have to reorganize and prioritize your schedule to make time to earn an extra income. The wise Stephen R. Covey says, "The key is not to prioritize what's on your schedule, but to schedule your priorities."

GET SUPPORT

Make sure that your spouse and children are on board. If they aren't supportive, you'll have a hard time making your business successful. Often, business opportunities present themselves as hobbies at first. Then, slowly they turn into a way to make money. At this point, you will need to re-evaluate with your spouse the expectations both of you have.

Is this something that you can start and run on your own? One of the biggest words of wisdom I can offer you is to choose wisely when deciding on a potential business partner. It becomes very rough water when you mix a friendship and a business. Someone you would choose to be your best friend may not be the same person with whom you would do business. If you can run this business by yourself, try it out. If it becomes too hard, then bring someone else in. If you start a business with a friend, make the terms very clear. Get everything in writing and specifically include what you expect from each person.

Don't give up. Release your inner Mom-preneur, and email us if you need a pep talk. You can do it!

For more advice on becoming debt-free and financially independent, we recommend:

The Total Money Makeover: A Proven Plan for Financial Fitness by Dave Ramsey (February, 2007)

Suze Orman's 2009 Action Plan by Suze Orman (December, 2008)

The Difference: How Anyone Can Prosper in Even The Toughest Times by Jean Chatzky (March, 2009)

CHAPTER FOURTEEN

Couponing to Thrive

Once you pay off your debt, the real fun begins. Just because you *can* pay full price for groceries doesn't mean you *should*! Use your brain, your time, and your savvy skills to improve your situation.

When I first started couponing, I had a very impatient husband. He wanted quick results, and he wasn't seeing them. I was having so much fun building my stockpile that I was spending almost the same amount each month on groceries as my pre-couponing days. My very skeptical sweetie saw me spending hours more a month on the computer, at the grocery store, organizing my binder, bragging to my friends, but he wasn't seeing me spend less money. He was worried. Suddenly, when our stockpile was established, we saw an enormous drop in our spending. After about three months, we were spending half of what we'd spent before. I can't even express how great it felt to realize how much room we'd just made in our budget.

At my house, our average savings runs between $600 and $800...PER MONTH. Here are a few examples from our monthly budget for a family of four. In April, I spent $286.15 on all my grocery shopping, including household shopping, cleaning supplies and toiletries. Without coupons, my total would have been $1,133.60. That's a savings of 76%. In May I spent $267.62 on all my shopping, and my total before coupons was $942.72, a savings of 72%. I did thirty-one transactions in May—yikes! That's like going to the store every day. (Don't worry, I didn't *actually* go to the store every day. I just did multiple transactions at a time). And those were big stockpiling months where I spent more than I usually do! June was more typical. I spent $117.01 on all my groceries, toiletries, produce meat—everything! My totals before coupons were $540.58, a savings of 78%.

I never kept a strict grocery budget before couponing, but between my weekly shopping trips, my late afternoon grocery runs, and my wholesale club massacres, my monthly grocery budget was around $500.00. I did my best to shop generics, sales and cook cost-effective meals, but my grocery budget still sat around $500 per month.

Now that I coupon, during a big spending month, I'm still spending only about half of my old grocery budget. The most beneficial result of couponing is my stockpile of food and toiletries worth many thousands of dollars. But my family also has an extra $250-$400 dollars in our pocket each month.

Once you have your stockpile and some extra money on hand every month, you're left with a decision. What do you do with all that extra money? It's tempting to take bi-annual trips to Tahiti or douse your home in Pottery Barn, but hang on a second. I love vacations, Pottery Barn (and don't forget my beloved Banana Republic), as much as anybody, but let's start thinking long term.

* *

Long-term Financial Independence

Sometimes you gotta get a little krazy to make a lasting change.

- If you have struggled with credit card debt, once your cards are paid off in full, CUT THEM UP. They are dead to you! Repeat after me: "I, _____, will NEVER use another credit card to buy something for which I don't have cash in the bank."

- Get rid of any other lingering debt like car payments or student loans. Get them out of your life, forever. For an average family this shouldn't take more than three years. Put vacations on hold, don't buy a new house or car, and put any extra money toward these debts. If you get a big bonus or tax return, pay off the car instead of driving to Vegas. You'll have plenty of time (and cash!) for road trips later.

- Stay the course. Once you become debt-free, the trick is to *stay* debt free. This means it's time to stockpile money. This way, if your car breaks, your dryer blows up, you need a new roof, or whatever surprise comes next, you won't need to borrow from your in-laws or even worse, a credit card company. You'll be able to meet unexpected expenses with ease.

Where is the best place to put your savings? A few options include:

Money Market Accounts

Great for money that needs to be accessible like your cash stockpile. It allows your money to earn a little interest at the same time. It's frequently suggested that you let your stockpile build in a money market account until it's enough money to sustain your family completely, including make your mortgage payment for 4-6 months.

401K

This is a retirement plan for employees of participating companies. Check with your employer to see if they offer this type of investment vehicle. Contributions to a 401K may be made with pre-tax dollars and often employers will match a maximum monthly contribution. 401K money will be taxed when you begin to take money out so it is not the ideal investment for money you may need prior to retirement age.

IRAs

Individual Retirement Accounts are another great way to save and grow your money long-term. You may contribute up to $5,000 per year (unless you're over fifty, then you may contribute $6,000). IRAs are another great way to avoid paying taxes as you're trying to save. In a traditional IRA you make pre-tax contributions, and much like a

401K, your money will only be taxed when you take it out. A Roth IRA is my family's personal savings preference. A Roth IRA allows you to contribute after-tax money, but then when you want to retire in twenty, thirty, or forty years you can withdraw the money tax-free! I love not giving the government more of my money almost as much as I love giving less of it to the grocery stores!

Invest in yourself

Invest your money in a personal small business, especially a business of your own. There is nothing you will want to succeed more than something into which you put sweat and money. Consider investing in your formal education. Take independent study or night classes and let your coupon savings pay the tuition!

Pay off your house

I dream of the day when I've completely paid for my home. I get a little giddy imagining writing the last check to my mortgage company. Once you have paid off all credit cards, student loans, and car loans, make it a priority to pay extra toward your mortgage. Even if you just send one or two hundred dollars extra each month, this will allow you to take years off your mortgage—years! Don't own your home? Start saving money each month to someday use as a down payment.

Save for college

Think about your kids' college. Whether your kids are fifteen or five or five months, you should be building some sort of college fund for them. The best option is an Educational Savings Account. This sort of account earns interest, and it is tax-FREE as long as it is used for Education. FREE!

● ●

BE HAPPY LIVING ON LESS

I love pretty things: furniture, picture frames, fireplaces, jetted tubs, jewelry, shoes, dessert, diamonds, Hawaiian vacations...you get the idea. Sure, living large *sounds* nice: strawberry daiquiris at the beach by day, pampering and ice cream by night, with handsome foreign men rubbing my perfectly manicured feet while I read ridiculous novels. But at the end of the day, all the treats would rot my teeth and I'd be spoiled and unhappy. What makes us truly happy are the people around us and our relationships with others. Money problems corrupt relationships and bring stress into the family home. My husband would spend himself into techno-oblivion if I didn't bring him back to reality, and my daughter would be dressed like Suri Cruise if he didn't do the same for me. At the same time Krazy Coupon Lady is not about deprivation. I'm not suggesting you move to a trailer and sell all your belongings just so you can be debt-free. If you save $400 in a month by couponing, why not spend $100 on a new pair of jeans and some earrings and invest the other portion? Or use the $400 to invest in yourself and a business venture you've always wanted to pursue?

I know for a fact that your wallet is going to be busting at the seams, and I want you to think about what you're going to do with that money. Put it to good use instead of blowing it all on something as perishable as groceries. Being a Krazy Coupon Lady is about a lot more than saving a few hundred a month on groceries. You will see your spending start to decrease in other areas as well. After you get into this coupon thing, your mind will experience a transformation, and you'll be unwilling to pay retail for anything, ever again! You'll be couponing yourself to dinner, the movies, vacation, and retirement!

Now, Stretch that Budget!

Now that you know how you need to handle your money, we want to share a few last ideas on how you can keep more money in your bank account. Build your cash stockpile more quickly and stretch it farther with the following great money saving and stockpiling tips. Some of these ideas will seem like common sense and others might be something you never considered, but either way, it's time to implement 'em.

My stockpile consists of much more than just food and toiletries...it's even taking over my husband's "man space" in the garage. The stockpiling principle is as simple as it sounds: buy something you're going to need, before you need it. Pay less and buy now instead of paying more when you "need it now." You might think you don't have room to store or deal with all this stockpiled stuff, but you'll be glad you created room. My family just moved 1,000 miles across the country, and I packed up cases and cases of my stockpile. Some people thought I'd gone crazy, but I would (and will!) do it again in a heartbeat.

More Stockpiles

STOCKPILE CHILDREN'S CLOTHING:

By now you know that a Krazy Coupon Lady never pays retail price. In order to get the best deals on my children's clothes, I always buy clothes on clearance, usually in a size up for the next year. If I buy a winter coat in September or October when the stores are just breaking them out, I could pay the full retail price of $49.50. But I wait and buy the exact coat in March for $9.97. I bought it a size up so this winter my daughter will have a brand new $50 coat. Coats should be your first priority when creating a stockpile of your children's clothes because they always need them, and they're easy to anticipate. Make sure to start stockpiling the necessities and work down to all the rest.

If I didn't spend a penny on clothes for the next twelve months, my kids would be so well-dressed no one would know the difference. Believe it or not, I have an entire year's worth of clothes boxed up in my garage. My three- or six-month cash emergency fund might last me a year when I have stockpiles of food, toiletries, AND clothes.

When my children outgrow their clothes, I either sell them or store them. My nicest, name brand outfits go on eBay. (Note: don't waste your time selling generic brand clothes on eBay because they won't sell). I often purchase name-brand clothing on clearance and end up selling it on eBay a year or two later for more than I paid for it in the first place! Take good pictures, provide accurate descriptions, and you'll be on your way to eBay success!

The other way I like to sell is at bi-annual consignment sales that allow you to set your own prices. Search for these consignment sales in your area, usually held in early spring (February or March) or fall (Usually October). You can set your own prices and hang your items on the racks at the sale. You usually keep about 70% of the profit from your clothes selling, and the rest pays for your participation in the sale. If I have a dress and I want at least $7.00 for it since I paid $12.00 (clearance price) when it was new, I price the dress at $10.00. When it sells, I get $7.00. If there aren't consignment sales like this in your community, consider starting a business! I also love to shop these sales. I have a keen eye for a bargain, and I buy many of my kids' goodies here.

* *

STOCKPILE GIFTS:

This is a GREAT way to save money. When I see a gift for my child on a clearance rack, or if I have a coupon, I buy it and hide it away. Shop after holiday sales for toys and pay 75% less than retail! When birthdays or Christmas come around, I rarely have to go buy something. I just pull gifts out of the gift stockpile cupboard.

Another money saver is to stockpile gifts for birthday parties of your kids' friends. If you're buying for a child under five, head to the dollar store. If you buy five presents, your son or daughter will be the coolest kid at the party, and you only paid $5.00 instead of $20.00.

I also stockpile adult gifts. I can stock up on Bath & Body Works when the soap is only a dollar or two, or shop Target's clearance section for vases or other nice gifts. If my friend has a birthday, I can still give her something thoughtful without breaking my monthly budget.

Stockpile wrapping paper, supplies, and cards. I buy a lot of these items at after holiday sales. I buy holiday wrapping paper and next year's Christmas cards on December 26th of the previous year. If you wait until December 30th, the selection is smaller, but you'll save even more! Try to buy plain paper, like a solid red, that you can use for birthdays or other occasions.

Nice baskets and cellophane are also worth stockpiling. Wedding and baby shower gifts add up quickly. Guess what I do now? I put together gift baskets that always receive rave reviews.

> For a baby shower: Diapers, wipes, baby shampoo, baby soap, baby lotion, and powder.

> For a wedding: Lysol cleaning supplies and wipes, toothbrushes, toothpaste, razors, shave gel, nice lotion, first aid kit, etc.

Give gift baskets to people with the basics of beginning their own stockpiles. It's better than the ugly crystal vase that they don't like and can't find where to return. These things will all save them money, and you can find them for almost-free.

STOCKPILE OFFICE AND SCHOOL SUPPLIES

Project what your school-aged child will need throughout the year and stockpile in August when the sales are huge. Stockpile printer ink and paper, scissors, pens, highlighters, paper clips, rubber-bands and more!

Need I go on? We could talk about stockpiling all day long because it's a principle that applies to almost everything. Don't stockpile electronics, cars, or couture clothing that will decrease significantly in value. But generally speaking, if you see a great deal on something you know you'll use, buy it when it's cheap and have it when you need it. Thinking ahead allows you to save big.

Other Thrifty Tips

COOKING AND EATING:

How can you meal plan and prepare meals on a budget now that you're a Krazy Coupon Lady?

- Continue to plan a menu: Plan a menu around the foods you know you have in surplus! Having a plan helps prevent me from eating out due to laziness. I try to have something started or thawing by 5:00 p.m. when the evil "Let's just go out" thoughts enter my mind. Why spend $30.00 on a regular dinner when I could buy a week's worth of food for that?

- Pack a lunch: If you work out of the home, pack a lunch. Even if you're eating on a budget and spending only $5.00 a day on lunch at work, that's at least $200 per month you can save if you'll pack your own lunch. If your spouse is eating out at work, lay down the law.

- Plant a Garden: a garden lowers your produce cost and serves as a fresh, convenient stockpile. Choose the vegetables you eat most often and plant away! Consider planting a few fruit trees or berry bushes for more snacking and even jam-making.

- Freeze ahead: After the birth of my first child, my mother came to take care of us, and when she cooked, she prepared food but also made freezer meals that were lifesavers after she was gone. Now, I often double my recipes, making one dish to eat tonight and freezing the other. This works best for casseroles, such as chicken pot-pie, enchiladas, or lasagna, but I also like to do it with big pots of soup. I put the soup in a gallon freezer bag and set that in a square Tupperware container until it freezes, then remove it. Few things are more beautiful than a freezer full of stacked casseroles and blocks of frozen soup.

SAVE ON MEAT

Meat is one of the most expensive things at the store! How to save more:

- Befriend the butcher! In the evenings, many grocery store butchers have a surplus of one of their meats. Stop by and ask whether he or she has any great deals.

- Buy in bulk. Find the best price per pound, and buy a family size portion. Then, take the meat home, divide it into portions for your family and freeze the portions for future use.

- Don't be too afraid of buying ground beef or lean beef instead of the "extra-extra-diet-lean!" Just make sure you drain the fat, and after you've done that, rinse your ground meat with <u>hot</u> water (use a colander if the holes aren't too big).

- Add beans to your meat to stretch it farther. I like to add black beans, kidneys, or pintos to my Mexican dishes in order to stretch the meat. I think it's really yummy, and it allows us to make a dish like taco salad, with half the ground beef I would normally use.

- Don't be afraid to buy sale meat! Just make sure you either cook it or throw it in the freezer when you get home. We've all seen those big orange $1 off or $2 off stickers on meat at the grocery store. My secret? Find the smallest package with the largest value off sticker. This week, I saw lots of orange stickers on the meat so I went to peruse. My best find was a small package of breakfast steaks. The largest breakfast steak package was priced at $4.79 and the smallest at $1.92, and they all had the same $1.00 off sticker. Buy the smaller package to get the better deal. I bought the small package with three small steaks for $0.92!

Miscellaneous Thrifty Tips:

- Entertainment: Borrow books and movies from the library. This is my kids' favorite weekly activity. They look forward to it every Thursday. I feel like Santa Claus because they can have whatever they want from the library and it's all free! We rarely spend money buying books or movies because we have an endless supply at the library.

- The car: Don't let it idle in the driveway for ten minutes in winter, and use AC sparingly in summer. Keep your oil changed and your tires inflated and rotated.

- Laundry: Dry your clothes using low heat. Wash laundry with cold water instead of warm or hot. Hang your clothes out to dry on sunny days.

- Around the house: Set your thermostat back a few degrees at night. Fix leaky faucets. Turn the heat dry option off on your dishwasher. Don't let the water run while you are brushing your teeth. Lower the temperature on your hot water heater. Install a low flow shower-head to cut back on water use.

- Monthly payments: Have satellite or cable TV? Find out what your friends are paying for the same service. Many cable providers will give you a lower rate just for calling in. Tell them if they don't charge you, say, $40 per month instead of $60, you'll go to another provider. It works almost every time.

- Don't pay the bank: Switch to a free checking account.

- Phone Bills: Decide whether to use a cell phone or a landline and get rid of the other one to save big. Consider using Skype, which allows you to make free calls via the Internet. Call from your computer to another computer for free, or choose from plans beginning at $2.95 per month!

Think about making your coupon savings a family event. Put the money in a jar earmarked for a family activity, trip, or big purchase. See how supportive your little grocery helpers and coupon clippers become when they're working toward bigger savings for the jar. Have your heart set on something just for you (how about a nice duvet cover from Pottery Barn, a favorite hardcover book, or some new MAC makeup)? Cut the picture out of the magazine and tape it to a jar, just for you! But wait, this is important. Talk to your spouse about keeping just 10-20% of your total coupon savings to buy whatever it is. The rest can go right in the joint account. Your spouse will very likely agree, and in a few months, you'll be knocking on the glass doors at the mall and waiting for them to open so you can go get what you've earned.

* *

Need a Recap?

Now that you understand how much fun (and money) couponing will add to your life, let's review.

To get started, you need to:

- *Be willing to set aside an hour or two each week.*

- *Collect multiple copies of coupons.*

  - With newspaper coupons, find a way (through extra subscriptions, neighbors or co-workers, or befriending the newspaper boy) to get at least four to six copies of your local Sunday paper.

  - Watch for the weekly store ads, often available in-store.

  - Online, you can buy newspaper coupons from eBay, print coupons from the Internet (visit TheKrazyCouponLady.com for a comprehensive list of current printable coupons), and find store coupons on the store's website.

  - Watch for peelies, tearpads, and blinkies in the store.

  - Keep your eyes and ears open for Catalina deals, both advertised and unadvertised.

- Don't be afraid to special order items or ask for rain checks if they sell out before you can make your purchase.

- *Organize your coupons.* Choose whichever binder method you find most appealing (organizing by date or organizing by category). Find the list of supplies you need to get started in Chapter 6. Put your contact information in your binder in case it gets lost, and bring it with you every time you go to the store.

- *Learn how to spot rock-bottom prices.* Never buy if the price isn't incredible. When you find a great deal, stock up! With perishable goods, purchase as many as you can reasonably use before they expire. With nonperishable goods like cleaners, buy as many as you'd like.

- *Learn store policies.* For stores you frequent, obtain your own copy of their policies and store it in your binder. Sit down and talk with local store management to make sure you're on the same page.

- *Get ready for checkout.* Choose wisely the time of day you head to the store. Try to go when it's slow so your cashier will be in a good mood, and there won't be a huge line behind you. Get organized before you leave the house, with separate lists for different transactions if necessary. If you have kids, take them to the store early in the morning or right after naptime. Feel free to "profile" and choose a cashier who looks coupon-friendly. Talk to your cashier before he or she begins ringing you up to see if he or she has a preference (coupons now or coupons later?) and don't be afraid to ask management to clarify if necessary.

Whew! Are you ready or what?? You can do it! Don't worry; if you're new to this, you'll be a pro in no time. With *Pick Another Checkout Lane, Honey*, there's nothing you can't have. Krazy Coupon Ladies can have our cake (at $0.25 a box of mix!) and eat it too, washed down with an ice-cold, dirt-cheap soda, and cleaned up with free paper towels if we spill. We sleep well at night with minty fresh breath (thanks to free toothpaste), knowing that we're in control of our financial futures, and awake to gourmet breakfast cereals we bought for next to nothing.

We know you'll love the rush you get from loading the car top to bottom with groceries you snagged at rock-bottom prices. If you still have questions or need a pep talk along the way, we're ready to guide and cheer you on to couponing success at TheKrazyCouponLady.com. Let us know what you decide to do with the $600-$800 per month you save, and send us a postcard on your next ritzy vacation made possible by careful coupon clipping. We can't wait to hear your success stories! Just don't tell us if your stockpile begins to gleam brighter than ours...we don't know whether we could take it.

Happy couponing!

You will be a Krazy Coupon Lady,
when you pay off your debts, command your
finances & coupon your way to prosperity.

CHAPTER FIFTEEN

Insider Tips:
SECRETS TO SAVE BIG AT TWENTY
STORES ACROSS THE NATION

Now that you've got the tools and you're ready to shop, how about a bit more guidance on where the best places may be to shop in your area? Below you will find insider secrets on how to maximize your savings at twenty of the best places in the nation to shop with coupons!

We're sure there are plenty of great stores in your area that are not on our list. We couldn't cover them all here. Follow the steps in Chapter 9 to acquire store policies for all your local stores! Flip back to Chapter 1 to review the different types of grocery stores and what to look for when choosing where to do your shopping!

Please note that while The Krazy Coupon Lady has used the most updated versions of the store policies as of the printing of this book, we are not responsible for any changes that stores implement. So it is recommended you still double check the store policies online or contact the stores to make sure you have the most recent versions. For the latest information visit TheKrazyCouponLady.com.

ALBERTSONS

Albertsons' regular prices are high, but their sales and promos are HOT!

Before you shop Albertsons with coupons, here's what you should know about its policy:

- Albertsons accepts newspaper, printable, and other manufacturer coupons.
- Albertsons runs promotions each week: You may use coupons on the items in these promotions to save even more!
- Albertsons sales typically run Wednesday to Tuesday.
- Select regions distribute store coupons in the weekly ad, which you may use with a manufacturer coupon.
- Select regions distribute "twice the value" coupons. This store coupon matches the value of a manufacturer coupon up to $1.00 off. A $1.00 off coupon will become $2.00 off, a $0.50 off coupon will become $1.00 off, a $1.50 off coupon will receive no special treatment.
- Select regions use a store loyalty card, or "preferred card." Ask you store and sign up!

THE SECRET
Stack coupons with Albertsons promotions!

Albertsons runs two kinds of promotions, the "Save Instantly" promo and the "On Your Next Order" promo.

First: the "Save Instantly" Promo
Example: Spend $20. Save $5 Instantly.
The register instantly deducts $5 after you spend $20 (total before coupons) on participating products and scan your preferred card. You may take advantage of this promo multiple times in one transaction. *Example: If you spend $40 on participating products, the register will deduct $10 (twice in $5 increments).*

Here is another example of a Save Instantly Promotion:

Spend $10 on Nabisco products, Save $3 Instantly
Buy 4 Nabisco Wheat Thins $2.50
Use 4 $1.00/1 Wheat Thins Coupons from the Smart Source coupon insert
Save $3 Instantly
Pay: $3.00 plus tax

Second: the "OYNO" Promo
Example: Spend $20, Save $5 on your next order (OYNO)
Your total before coupons is $20. Then present any coupons and pay. With your receipt your cashier will hand you a Catalina coupon worth $5.00 off your next order. These Catalinas can be rolled. This means you can do one transaction, receive the Catalina, do another identical transaction, pay with the first Catalina, and a new Catalina will still print. Often, OYNO promos can potentially be "moneymakers."

Example: Lunchables $2.79
Use $1.00/1 manufacturer coupon
Pay: $1.79, receive a $1 Catalina to use another on your next order

You could roll this Catalina and buy another Lunchables. Then you would only pay $0.79 out of pocket, and still receive a new $1 Catalina.

Albertsons Coupon Policy:

Manufacturer Coupons: Coupons issued by the manufacturer containing: "terms of agreement," face value, expiration date, and verbiage "manufacturer coupon." They have handling instructions printed on them.

Most manufacturer coupons have barcodes on them and can be scanned. Any coupons that do not scan or do not have barcodes should be checked for validity of expiration date and purchase requirements.

Albertsons may issue coupons that are manufacturer coupons that contain the words "redeemable only at Albertsons."

Store Coupons: Company's discount offers in various forms of media including, but not limited to, print, electronic, newspaper, direct mailers, kiosks, and Company websites.

Store coupons may also contain the words "redeemable only at Albertsons" (or a banner of Albertsons).

Store coupons may state that the discount applies only with Preferred Card/Super Card/Loyalty Card.

When redeeming a store coupon, the terms printed on the coupon must be adhered to.

Catalina Checkout Coupons/Rebates: Catalina is a third party vendor that partners with vendors and Albertsons to offer both manufacturer coupons and Albertsons in-store coupons. When you purchase qualified items at checkout, it triggers the Catalina printer to generate a coupon.

It is Albertsons' policy that these coupons are to be used in a future purchase, not within the purchase in which they are generated.

Catalina coupons can only be given to the customer for whom they were intended (not to any other customer or associate). If a customer does not want his or her Catalina coupons, it is Albertsons' policy that the cashier destroys them immediately.

Catalina may be contacted at 1-888-826-8766 for any questions about redemption and\or if a coupon fails to print within a transaction.

Albertsons will NOT accept printable coupons for "Free" product not requiring purchase, for value which exceeds $5.00, for coupons lacking a UPC bar code or photocopied printable coupons.

In order to provide better values for its customers and to continue to deliver the best pricing possible in its weekly ads, Albertsons has discontinued the acceptance of competitor's coupons. Albertsons is the last retail grocer in most of our operating areas to discontinue this practice.

BJ's Wholesale Club

Before you shop BJ's with coupons, here's what you should know about its policy:

- BJ's is the only Wholesale club that accepts all manufacturer coupons. When paired with items that are marked down or deeply discounted, you can save big.
- BJ's is a members only wholesale club. Membership currently costs $45 annually.
- BJ's accepts newspaper, printable, and other manufacturer coupons.
- BJ's distributes store coupons via BJs.com, BJ's member magazine, BJ's mailers, and BJ's in-club coupon fliers.
- Select BJ's Clubs will accept one store coupon and one manufacturer coupon per item.

The Secret

Shop BJ's low prices and use store and manufacturer coupons together to maximize savings!

At BJ's, if you buy a multipack, you can use multiple manufacturer coupons. For example, if you buy a twelve-pack of mandarin oranges and each can has its own barcode, you can use twelve manufacturer coupons on that purchase.

Example: Filippo Berio Olive Oil, Extra Virgin 2-2liter $17.89
Use two $2/1 coupons from the Smart Source coupon insert
Final Price: $13.89, or $6.95/2 liter

CVS

Before you shop CVS with coupons, here's what you need to know:

- CVS accepts both newspaper, printable, and other manufacturer coupons.
- CVS weekly sales run Sunday to Saturday.
- CVS tracks your purchases and Extra Bucks rewards through your CVS Extra Care card. Make sure you apply for a card!
- CVS has weekly sales ads as well as weekly and monthly "Extra Bucks" promotions. Extra bucks are coupons worth a $ amount off your next purchase, similar to Catalinas. Extra Bucks print at the bottom of your receipt and expire exactly four weeks after printed.
  Example of an Extra Bucks promo: Spend $15 on participating candy products, receive $5 Extra Bucks. You must only spend $15 subtotal, before coupons!

- Extra Buck offers have limits per card.
- CVS has great store coupons that print on the bottom of your receipt just like Extra Bucks. An example store coupon could be $1.00 off any deodorant, and it will also expire four weeks after print.
- CVS has purchase based coupons: common values include $2 off $10 purchase, $3 off $15, $4 off $20, $5 off $30 etc. These purchase based coupons expire the most quickly, around two weeks after printed.

THE SECRET

Stack manufacturer coupons with store coupons on an "extra bucks" promo item!
Then, get a few deals like the one below. Do them in one transaction and
add a purchase-based coupon such as $3 off $15 and save even more!

Example: Old Spice Deodorant on sale $3.49
Buy 1 Old Spice, receive $1.49 Extra Buck
Use $1.00 off any deodorant CVS store coupon
Use $1.00 off Old Spice deodorant manufacturer coupon
Pay $1.49, receive $1.49 Extra Buck

Final Price: Free!

This deal could be even sweeter if you had extra bucks to offset your out-of-pocket expense. If you'd had a $1.00 Extra Buck, you could have used it as well and paid $0.49. You would still receive the $1.49 Extra Buck!

Food Lion

Before you shop Food Lion with coupons, here's what you should know about its policy:

- We will only accept coupons that are in date and the product or purchase requirements have been met.
- Competitor coupons will not be accepted in our stores.
- We will accept Manufacturer, Store, Internet and Catalina Checkout Coupons.
- Coupons with limits specified on them must be followed.
- No "cash back" will be given for coupons of any kind.
- Customers may not use more than (1) one coupon per item with a maximum of (10) ten coupons for the same item per customer.
- We will only accept Internet coupons that appear to be originals.
- We will not accept internet coupons from other retailers.
- We will not accept FREE internet coupons.
- We will accept Manufacturer and Store coupons for FREE items.
- The value of the FREE item cannot exceed the purchase price of that item.
- We reserve the right to limit the quantity of coupons that may be redeemed in one shopping visit. We also reserve the right to refuse any coupon that may appear to be fraudulent.

The Secret

Combine a sale priced item with a manufacturer coupon and
a Food Lion printable coupon to maximize savings

Example:

Huggies Pure & Natural, $9.97
Use 1 $3.00/1 Huggies Pure & Natural Diapers Manufacturer Coupon
Use 1 $1.50/1 Food Lion Internet Printable Coupon
Final Price: $5.47 after both coupons

GIANT EAGLE

Before you shop Giant Eagle with coupons, here's what you should know about its policy:

- Giant Eagle accepts newspaper, printable, and other manufacturer coupons.
- Store Sales run Thursday to Wednesday.
- You must use the store loyalty card to get sale prices.
- Select Giant Eagle stores double coupons up to 99 cents.
- Giant Eagle stores have Catalina Promotions (both advertised and unadvertised).
- Giant Eagle has store coupons that you can usually combine with manufacturer coupons.
- Select Giant Eagle stores double coupons up to $0.99 in Value.
- 1 coupon per item(s) purchased as stated on the coupon with a maximum of 12 coupons per same 12 items purchased.
- Coupon value cannot exceed the price of the item(s) purchased.
- If you forget to use your coupons at the time of purchase, we will accept them with your receipt and Giant Eagle Advantage Card® up to 7 days beyond the date on the receipt.

THE SECRET
Stack store coupons, manufacturer coupons, and a promo if you can!

Giant Eagle runs two kinds of promotions, The "Save Instantly" promo and The "On Your Next Order" promo

First: the "Save Instantly" Promo
Example: Spend $10, Save $2 Instantly.
The register instantly deducts $2 after you spend $10 (total before coupons) on participating products. You may take advantage of this promo multiple times in one transaction. Meaning, if you spend $20 on participating products, the register will deduct $40 (twice in $2 increments).

Second: the "OYNO" Promo
Example: Spend $20, Save $5 on your next order (OYNO)
Your total before coupons is $20, then redeem any coupons and pay. With your receipt your cashier will hand you a long, receipt-like Catalina coupon worth $5.00 off your next order. These Catalinas can be rolled. This means you can do one transaction, receive the Catalina, do another identical transaction, pay with the first Catalina and a new Catalina will still print.

Example Promo: Buy 5 Post Cereals, save $5 on your next order
Buy 5 Post Cereals $2.00 each
Use 5 $1.00/1 Manufacturer Coupons
Save $5 on your next order
Final Price: Free

Harris Teeter

Before you shop Harris Teeter with coupons, here's what you should know about its policy:

- Harris Teeter accepts newspaper, printable, and other manufacturer coupons.
- Harris Teeter uses a store loyalty card, called VIC for Very Important Customer. Apply in store so you can get the lowest sale prices and double your coupons.
- Harris Teeter sales run Wednesday to Tuesday.
- Harris Teeter accepts competitor coupons.
- Harris Teeter doubles coupons up to $0.99 in value, and up to twenty per day. Additionally, you can only double three coupons for the same item.
- Select Harris Teeter locations have Triple Coupon Events. (These are the times where you pull out a map and consider a road trip just to get to the deals!)

The Secret
Shop promotions and double your coupons for maximum savings!

Harris Teeter runs two kinds of promotions:

First: the "Save Instantly" Promo

Example: Spend $20, Save $5 Instantly.

The register instantly deducts $5 after you spend $20 (total before coupons) on participating products and scan your VIC card. You may take advantage of this promo multiple times in one transaction. Meaning, if you spend $40 on participating products, the register will deduct $10 (twice in $5 increments).

Spend $15 on GM products, save $5 instantly
Buy 5 Green Giant Frozen Vegetables $1.00
Buy 4 Betty Crocker Frosting $1.25
Buy 3 Betty Crocker Warm Delights $1.67
Use 5 $0.25/1 Green Giant coupons
Use 4 $0.50/1 Betty Crocker Frosting coupons
Use 3 $0.50/1 Betty Crocker warm delights
Save $5 instantly
Final Price: $5.25 or $0.58 per item

This deal could be even sweeter if you doubled or tripled your coupons!

Second: the "OYNO" Promo
Example: Spend $20, Save $5 on your next order (OYNO)
Your total before coupons is $20, then redeem any coupons and pay. With your receipt your cashier will hand you a long, receipt-like Catalina coupon worth $5.00 off your next order. These Catalinas can be rolled. This means you can do one transaction, receive the Catalina, do another identical transaction, pay with the first Catalina, and a new Catalina will still print.

Harris Teeter Coupon Acceptance Policy

General

- We accept coupons that have not passed their expiration date for use; we cannot accept any expired coupons.
- We accept only one manufacturer coupon per purchased item.
- We do not accept coupons on items not purchased.
- Coupons must be presented at time of purchase; we cannot return money for coupons not used.
- Coupons presented and items purchased must match exactly; size, variety, flavor, etc.
- We uphold any purchase stipulations set forth by product manufacturer.
- We accept only one coupon for Buy One Get One Free items.
- We accept coupons for items only of equal or more value; we do not give cash back.
- Sales tax is paid by customer at full retail.

Doubling

- We accept 20 double coupons per day per customer/household with VIC card; all others redeemed at face value. No orders may be separated that would allow the 20 coupon limit to be exceeded.
- We double manufacturer's coupons up to face value of $0.99; with total amount not to exceed $1.98 or entire retail of item; whichever is less.
- We double up to three identical items with manufacturer coupon; additional coupons for like item will be honored at face value.
- No competitor coupons will be doubled or tripled.
- In the event of triple coupons, up to 20 coupons will be tripled per day per customer/household with VIC card; all others redeemed at face value. No orders may be separated that would allow the 20 coupon limit to be exceeded.

Internet Coupons

- We gladly accept Internet manufacturer's coupons for product; however no "free" product Internet coupons are accepted.
- With the purchase of two like manufacturer's products, we accept two Internet coupons, per store, per day.
- We do not accept Internet coupons that do not appear to be originals or that won't scan.

Competitor's Coupons

- We gladly accept local competitors' circular or direct-mail coupons for MONEY OFF THE TOTAL ORDER; we do not take competitor's coupons for money off specific items.
- We do not accept any Internet coupons from other retailers.

Rainchecks

- Rainchecks never expire and are accepted at any Harris Teeter store.
- We do not issue rainchecks for coupon items that may be out of stock or for "while supplies last" items.
- We reserve the right to limit raincheck quantities based on product availability and advertised limits.
- Rainchecks can be written for a limit of three unless otherwise stated in the ad.

Scan Guarantee

- Our scan guarantee states, "If an item scans higher than the shelf tag or sign, you will receive one like item free, excluding alcohol and tobacco."

Hy-Vee

Before you shop Hy-Vee with coupons, here's what you should know about its policy:

- Hy-vee accepts newspaper and Internet printable manufacturer coupons.
- Hy-vee accepts one store coupon and one manufacturer coupon on one item.
- Hy-Vee distributes great store coupons in its weekly ad and via Hy-Vee.com.
- Hy-Vee has Catalina machines and promotions.

The Secret
Stack store and manufacturer coupons with a sale price!

Example: Biz Laundry Detergent $4.99
$1.00/1 Hy-Vee printable store coupon
$1.50/1 Manufacturer coupon
Final Price: $2.49

Hy-Vee Official Coupon Policy

- The coupon must be legible.
- The coupon should have a scannable bar code (UPC) and a remittable manufacturer's address.
- Coupons must have an expiration date and must be used within the stated time frame. Expired coupons will not be accepted.
- Only one vendor coupon per item will be accepted. However, a customer may use a vendor coupon in combination with a Hy-Vee coupon on the same item.
- Coupon values that exceed the price of the item will not be accepted.
- Soft drink container caps will be accepted.

Due to increased fraud, the following two additional rules apply to internet coupons:

- Vendor coupons that involve any kind of free product will not be accepted, including "buy one, get one free" offers.
- A Store Director has authority to set monetary limitations (for example, $2.50 per coupon) for the acceptance of internet coupons at the Store Director's store.

KMART

Before you shop Kmart with coupons, here's some information on the policy:

- Kmart's regular prices are fairly high, but they have weekly sales and select regions occasionally double coupons!
- Kmart accepts newspaper, printable, and other manufacturer coupons.
- Kmart store coupons may print at the bottom of your receipt, or you may receive purchase based coupons, such as $10 off $50 by signing up for Kmart emails.
- Kmart does offer some promotions such as Spend $15 on participating products, receive $3 off your next order.
- Kmart only allows one coupon per product. You cannot use a store and manufacturer coupon together.
- Kmart sales run Sunday to Saturday.

THE SECRET
Combine double coupon days with in-store promotions!

Kmart Double Coupon Days is advertised in select regions on a fairly random basis. Double coupons run for an entire week: Sunday to Saturday. Coupons up to a certain value are doubled automatically by the register. For example: when Kmart doubles coupons up to $2.00, present your $2.00 coupon and receive $4.00 off. Coupons valued at $2.01 or above will not be doubled. Kmart usually sets a limit on how many coupons may be doubled per day.

Combine Kmart Double Days with a Catalina Promotion

Example: Dry Idea Deodorant $4.49 each
Buy 2, Earn a $2 Catalina to use on your next order
Use 2 $2.00/1 Dry Idea Printable Coupons; $2 coupon will be doubled to $4 off automatically by the register.
Final Price $0.98 Out of Pocket, Receive a $2 Catalina

Even though you pay $.98 Out of Pocket, we call this a moneymaker after factoring in the $2 Catalina.

KROGER

Before you shop at Kroger with coupons, here's a little information about its policy:

- Kroger accepts both newspaper, printable, and other manufacturer coupons. Printable Coupons must have a scannable barcode, a "bill to:" or "send to:" address in the fine print, and a valid, future expiration date.
- Kroger has weekly sales and promos, including Catalina promotions.
- Kroger's weekly sales usually run Wednesday to Tuesday, but in some regions run Thursday to Wednesday or Sunday to Saturday.
- Kroger also accepts eCoupons. Load them directly to your Kroger card!
- You must use a Kroger card to get store savings. You can sign up at the store's customer service desk.

THE SECRET

Shop Kroger promotions with coupons, and double coupons where you can!

Kroger Double Coupons:

Select Kroger stores double coupons up to $0.99. Kroger usually will not allow you to double more than one of the same coupon. This means if you buy four boxes of cereal, and use four $0.75 off coupons, they will only double one of those coupons. The rest of the coupons used, will be redeemed at face value.

In some regions, only the first eight coupons will be doubled; other regions have no limit.

Kroger Promotions:

- Kroger stores run "Save Instantly" promotions. The most common is a Buy 10 items, Save $5 Instantly.
- The Promo: Buy 10 Progresso soups, Save $5 instantly
Example: Buy 10 Progresso Soup $1.50 each
Use 1 $0.75/1 soup coupon (doubled)

Use 9 more $0.75/1 soup coupons (not doubled)
Save $5 instantly
Final Price: $1.75 or $0.17 per can of soup

Meijer

Before you shop Meijer with coupons, here's some information on the policy:

- Meijer accepts both newspaper, printable, and other manufacturer coupons.
- Meijer has weekly sales and promos, including Catalina promotions.
- Meijer weekly sales usually run Sunday to Saturday but in some regions run Wednesday to Tuesday.
- Meijer has great store coupons found largely at MeijerMealbox.com.
- Select Meijer locations double coupons. Most double coupons up to $0.50 in value, so a $0.35 coupon is worth $0.70 off, a $0.50 off coupon is worth $1.00 off.

THE SECRET

Stack store coupons from Meijer Mealbox, manufacturer coupons, and sale prices!

Example: Mt. Olive Pickles, $1.67
Use 2 $0.50/1 from 8/16 SS insert
And use $1.00/2 printable coupon from Meijer
Final Price: $0.17 each, when you buy 2

MEIJER OFFICIAL COUPON POLICY

- We accept two kinds of coupons; Meijer issued coupons and manufacturer coupons.
- Only one manufacturer coupon and one Meijer coupon for the same item will be accepted (unless prohibited).
- Mealbox coupons are considered Meijer coupons.
- We accept all valid internet coupons. See store for details.
- We reserve the right to limit quantities.
- If the value of the coupon is more than the price of the item after discounts or coupons are applied, the value of the coupon will be applied up to the price of the item.
- We do not apply the excess value of a coupon to the order total if the value of the coupon is over the price of the item after discounts or coupons are applied.
- Only coupons for products carried in our stores will be accepted.
- All coupons should be given to the cashier while you're checking out and cannot be applied to a previous purchase.

Publix

Before you shop Publix with coupons, here's what you should know about its policy:

- Publix accepts newspaper, printable, and other manufacturer coupons.
- Publix has store coupons, which can be used with manufacturer coupons.
- Publix has a bi-monthly Advantage Buy flier. In these fliers, you will find manufacturer and store coupons.
- Publix accepts competitor coupons, such as grocery store issued coupons, like Super Target coupons. Typically Publix will not accept drug store coupons from Walgreens or CVS, but you may ask your manager whether they are considered a competitor.
- Select Publix stores distribute coupons found in the Sunday Publix circular for Penny or Mystery Items. Sometimes they may get sneaky and put the penny item coupon somewhere else in the Sunday paper. These coupons are valid on Sunday and Monday only and are for select items and sizes. Usually there is a limit of one offer per customer, and you must spend $10 on other purchases. The $10 purchase is the total before coupons, so use coupons to get your out-of-pocket-expense down.
- Select Publix stores double coupons. Most of these participating stores will match the value of the coupon up to $0.50.

The Secret

Combine a sale price with a manufacturer coupon that can be doubled
and stack with a competitor's store coupon.

Example:
General Mills Cereal Buy 1 Get 1 Free at $3.79 each
Use (2) $.50/1 Manufacturer coupon from the Red Plum coupon insert (an additional $1 will be deducted for the Double)
Stack with a $1.50/2 General Mills Super Target Printable Coupon
Final Price: $0.29 or $0.15 each

RITE AID

Before you shop Rite Aid with coupons, here's some information on the policy:

- The best deals at Rite Aid utilize the Single Check Rebate (SCR) system. Rite Aid sends you a monthly check for the total of all your rebates purchased during that month. You can cash it as you would any other check.
- Rite Aid accepts newspaper, printable, and other manufacturer coupons.
- Rite Aid sales run Sunday to Saturday.

THE SECRET

Stack coupons with rebate items and get items for very cheap or free. You can even "make money" at Rite Aid. Often Rite Aid advertises an item as "Free after Rebate" in its Sunday ad.

Example: Let's say this month's rebate booklet contains a rebate of $2.49 for Scotch packing tape. And in Sunday's ad, you notice Scotch packing tape on sale for $2.49. There is a manufacturer coupon worth $1.00/1 Scotch product. Here's how this scenario would go:

Buy 1 Scotch packing tape $2.49
Use $1.00/1 Scotch product manufacturer coupon
Pay $1.49+tax
Submit for the rebate and receive $2.49 at the end of the month. You just made $1.00!

Rite Aid's detailed coupon policy can be found at RiteAid.com. Summary below:

More than one coupon can be used on the purchase of a single item under the following conditions:

- All coupons match the item being purchased.
- The total of the coupons is equal to or less than the selling price of the item before sales tax.
- No more than one Rite Aid Valuable coupon, one Rite Aid Manufacturer coupon, and one Manufacturer coupon can be used on a single item.
-

Buy One, Get One Free

We accept two coupons for the purchase of two items that are on Buy One, Get One Free Promotion.

We accept a Buy One, Get One Free Coupon with an item that is in our flyer as Buy One, Get One Free, meaning both items are free. The cash register will compute any sales tax due, which varies by state law.

SAFEWAY

Before you shop Safeway (or Safeway affiliate stores which include: Carrs, Dominick's, Genuardi's, Pavilions, Randalls, Tom Thumb and Vons), here's some information on the policy:

- Safeway accepts newspaper, printable, and other manufacturer coupons.
- Safeway store sales run from Wednesday to Tuesday.
- Safeway has store coupons, both in ad "Super Coupons" that require a minimum $10 purchase to qualify and printable coupons from Safeway.com. Safeway allows both a store and manufacturer coupon to be used per item.
- Safeway requires a Store Loyalty card, so sign up at the register or customer service desk!
- Safeway also accepts eCoupons. Load them directly to your Safeway club card!
- Safeway runs promotions each week.
- Safeway doubles coupons in select regions, usually up to $0.50.

THE SECRET

Use coupons, both store and manufacturer, on these promotions to maximize savings!

Safeway runs two kinds of promotions, the "Save Instantly" promo and the "On Your Next Order" promo.

First: the "Save Instantly" Promo

Example: Buy 5, Save $5 Instantly.

The register instantly deducts $5 after you buy five participating products and scan your Safeway club card. You may take advantage of this promo multiple times in one transaction. Meaning, if you buy ten products, the register will deduct $10 (twice in $5 increments).

Example Promo:

Buy 5 Welch's Grape Juice, save $5 instantly

Buy 5 Welch's Grape Juice $3.49 each
Use 5 $2.00/1 Manufacturer Coupons
Save $5 instantly
Final Price: $2.45 or $0.49 each

Second: the "OYNO" Promo

Example: Spend $30, Save $15 on your next order (OYNO)

Your total before coupons is $30, then redeem any coupons and pay. With your receipt, your cashier will hand you a long, receipt-like Catalina coupon worth $15.00 off your next order. These Catalinas can be rolled. This means you can do one transaction, receive the Catalina, do another identical transaction, pay with the first Catalina, and a new Catalina will still print.

SMITH'S

Before you shop Smith's with coupons, here's what you should know about its policy:

- Smith's accepts newspaper, printable, and other manufacturer coupons.
- You will need a Smith's Fresh Values card to obtain in store savings and sales.
- Smith's accepts eCoupons as part of the Kroger family. Load Smith's coupons to your Fresh Values card, under the Kroger links.
- Smith's sales run from Wednesday to Tuesday.
- Smith's runs promotions each week.
- Smith's runs two kinds of promotions, the "Save Instantly" promo and the "On Your Next Order" promo.

First: the "Save Instantly" Promo
Example: Buy 10 select products, Save $5 Instantly
The register instantly deducts $5 after you buy ten participating products and scan your Smith's Fresh Values card. You may take advantage of this promo multiple times in one transaction, meaning if you buy twenty participating products, the register will deduct $10 (twice in $5 increments).

Example: Nestle/Kraft Promo: Buy 10 Items, Get $5 off Instantly, Mix or Match
Buy 5 Juicy Juice, 64 oz or 8 ct $2.49
Buy 5 Nabisco Wheat Thins $2.20
Use 5 $1.00/1 manufacturer coupon
Use 5 $1.00/1 manufacturer coupon
Save $5 instantly
Final Price: $8.45 or $0.85 per item

Second: the "OYNO" Promo
Example: Spend $20, Save $5 on your next order (OYNO)
Your total before coupons is $20. Then redeem any coupons and pay. With your receipt, your cashier will hand you a long, receipt-like Catalina coupon worth $5.00 off your next order. These Catalinas can be rolled. This means you can do one transaction, receive the Catalina, do another identical transaction, pay with the first Catalina, and a new Catalina will still print.

STOP N SHOP

Before you shop Stop N Shop with coupons, here's what you should know about its policy:

- Stop N Shop accepts newspaper, printable, and other manufacturer coupons.
- At Stop N Shop, you can use one store coupon and one manufacturer coupon on one item.
- Stop N Shop runs Catalina promotions.
- You will need a Stop N Shop Customer Card to get savings and sales.
- Weekly sales run from Friday to Thursday.

Stop N Shop double coupons:
- Select Stop N Shop Stores double coupons up to $0.99 in value.
- Catalina coupons cannot be doubled.
- You can only double four coupons for identical items and up to sixteen of the same coupon. For example, if you have twenty General Mills Cereal coupons, only sixteen of them will be doubled, and you can only buy up to four identical cereals. You could buy four Trix, four Cocoa Puffs, four Kix and four Cheerios.

THE SECRET
Stack sale prices with manufacturer coupons, double coupons and promotions!

Example: Reese's Peanut Butter Cups minis $1.25
$0.55/1 manufacturer coupon (doubled)
Final Price: $0.15

Stop N Shop runs two kinds of promotions, the "Save Instantly" promo and the "On Your Next Order" promo.

First: the "Save Instantly" Promo
Example: Spend $25, Save $10 Instantly.

The register instantly deducts $10 after you spend $25 (total before coupons) on participating products and scan your Stop N Shop customer card. You may take advantage of this promo multiple times in one transaction. Meaning, if you spend $50 on participating products, the register will deduct $20 (twice in $10 increments).

Second: the "OYNO" Promo
Example: Spend $10, Save $3 on your next order (OYNO)

Your total before coupons is $10, then redeem any coupons and pay. With your receipt your cashier will hand you a long, receipt-like Catalina coupon worth $3.00 off your next order. These Catalinas can be rolled. This means you can do one transaction, receive the Catalina, do another identical transaction, pay with the first Catalina, and a new Catalina will still print.

TARGET

Before you shop Target with coupons, here's some information on the policy:

- Target accepts newspaper, printable, and other manufacturer coupons.
- Target Price matches: bring in a competitor ad and Target will match the price of the product as long as it's an exact match.
- Target runs gift card promotions: an example is "Buy 5 Kashi items, receive a $5 Target gift card." You may use coupons on these items and your result will be great savings! You do not have to separate your transactions. If you buy ten Kashi items, you'll receive two $5 gift cards, etc.
- Target has store coupons available at Target.com or occasionally available in your Sunday coupon inserts. You can print as many of these coupons as you like and use them at Target stores or anywhere that accepts competitor coupons. Target store coupons read: Limit one per transaction. You may do separate transactions.
- Target sales run Sunday through Saturday.

THE SECRET

Combine a gift card promotion with store and manufacturer coupons;
add a price match to the mix and now you're really krazy.

Example:Buy 5 Kashi products $2.88 each, receive $5 gift card
Price Match, take your local grocer ad that has Kashi products priced at $2.33
Use 5 $0.75/1 Kashi product Manufacturer coupons
Pay $1.58 per item, or $7.90 total, then receive a $5 gift card
Final Price: $2.90 or $0.58 per item after factoring gift card savings.

Target Coupon Policy, (available for print at Target.com):

Coupons are a great way to save even more when shopping with us, and it's easy to use them at our stores.

- Target accepts one manufacturer coupon and one Target coupon for the same item (unless prohibited)
- Super Target coupons can be used in any Target store if the store carries the item
- We gladly accept valid internet coupons

Because of the variety of coupons available to our guests, we do have some guidelines for how coupons can be redeemed at Target.

When accepting coupons, we use the following guidelines:

- We accept two kinds of coupons: Target-issued coupons and manufacturer-issued.
- We'll accept one Target coupon and one manufacturer coupon for the same item, unless either coupon prohibits it.
- Coupon amount may be reduced if it exceeds the value of the item after other discounts or coupons are applied.
- We can't give cash back if the face value of a coupon is greater than the purchase value of the item.
- We can't accept coupons from other retailers, or coupons for products not carried in our stores.
- All valid coupons should be presented to the cashier while you're checking out.

WALGREENS

Before you shop Walgreens with coupons, here's some information on the policy:

- Walgreens accepts newspaper, printable, and other manufacturer coupons.
- Walgreens has a great "Register Reward" Program. A Register Reward is a type of Catalina coupon that prints after you make a qualifying purchase. It is typically good for "X" amount off of your next purchase. When you purchase the qualifying item, you will receive a Register Reward to use on your next purchase.
- Walgreens has store coupons available in its weekly ad.
- At Walgreens, you can use one manufacturer coupon and one store coupon on one item, as long as neither coupon prohibits it.
- Walgreens sales run Sunday to Saturday.
- Managers can limit the number of sale items that you buy in a shopping trip.

THE SECRET

Combine a Sale Price with a Register Reward and a manufacturer coupon.

Example: True North Nut Crisps or Clusters $3.00

Buy 1, Earn a $2.00 Register Reward

Use the $1.00/1 True North Product printable coupon, or combine.

Pay $2.00 Out of Pocket, and receive the $2.00 Register Reward.

Even though you had to pay $2.00 out of pocket, we call this product "free."

Questions about Register Rewards:

Q. Can I buy two True North products and receive two Register Rewards?

A. No, only one Register Reward will print per transaction. You may buy True North nuts and a tube of toothpaste that also has a Register Reward, and you will be eligible to receive two Register Rewards from one transaction. The best way to buy two True North nuts is to do it in two separate transactions to receive two Register Rewards.

Q. Can I use the RR that I received from my first True North Nuts to pay for my next True North nuts?

A. This is known as "rolling" and cannot be done if you want another Register Reward to print. The best way to get around this, and keep the out-of-pocket expense low, is to find two different products that trigger the same value Register Reward and alternate buying those items in separate transactions, paying for the second transaction with the first Register Reward, and so forth.

Q. Can I pay for one item with a manufacturer coupon and a Register Reward?

A. At Walgreens, its registers will not allow you to have more coupons than items. This includes manufacturer coupons and Register Rewards. If you purchase one item and want to pay with one manufacturer coupon and one Register Reward, you will need to add a "filler" item. Before you checkout, do a quick count of your items and coupons. Make sure that you have at least one more item than you do coupons. When choosing a filler item, consider a clearanced item, pack of gum, individual caramel, or Sunday newspaper.

WALMART

Before you shop Walmart with coupons, here's some information on its policy:

- Walmart accepts newspaper, printable, and other manufacturer coupons.
- Walmart has everyday low prices as well as roll back prices.
- Walmart price matches: bring in the competitor ad to your store.
- Walmart accepts competitor coupons: bring in competing store coupons to your store.
- Walmart does not run many promotions or release a weekly grocery ad on a regular basis. Prices and sales tend to vary greatly by region.
- Walmart does not have consistent enforcement of any portion of its coupon policy. Some shoppers have a great experience at Walmart while others have quite the opposite.
- Walmart does not allow more than one coupon of any kind for one item. You may not use a store coupon and a manufacturer coupon together.

THE SECRET
Combine coupons with Walmart rollback prices. Or bring all your store ads
and coupons to Walmart and do a scenario like this:

Breyers Ice Cream 2 for $5.00 in Walgreens Drugstore weekly ad
$1.00/1 Breyers product, printable manufacturer coupon
Final Price at Walmart: $1.50 each

or

Breyer's Ice Cream 2 for $5.00 in Walgreens Drugstore weekly ad
$0.75/1 Breyers product, store coupon from Albertsons grocery ad
Final Price at Walmart: $1.75 each

Will Walmart accept any competitor coupon?

Walmart accepts valid "cents off" coupons from competing stores. "Cents off" means the coupon is worth $0.40 off or $2.00 off, etc. Walmart does not accept competitor coupons for a percentage off.

Will Walmart accept a coupon worth more than the product? $1.00 off coupon for $0.97 product?

Walmart should accept the coupon and adjust it down to the value of the item.

Can I use a store's competitor coupon and a manufacturer coupon on one item?

No. Walmart's policy states one coupon per item. In this case, you will need to choose one of the two coupons.

If you have problems with policy, call 1.800.Walmart while still in the store.

Walmart's Coupon Policy

Walmart accepts the following types of coupons (see guidelines below):

- Manufacturer coupons (Cents Off)
- Free merchandise (or manufacturer's Buy-One-Get-One-Free) coupons
- Store coupons
- Pharmacy (Advertising and Promotional) coupons
- Internet coupons
- Soft drink container caps

The following are guidelines and limits:

- Walmart only accepts coupons for merchandise we sell and only when presented at the time of purchase.
- Coupons should have an expiration date and be presented within the valid dates. Walmart will not accept expired coupons.
- Internet coupons should be legible and say "Manufacturer Coupon." There should be a valid remit address for the manufacturer and a scannable bar code.
- Only one coupon per item is permitted.
- Use of forty or more coupons per transaction will require approval by Customer Service Manager.

Walmart Price Matching

Our goal is always to be the low price leader in every community where we operate. Our customers trust us to have everyday low prices...there's no need for "special sales."

Our unbeatable promise:

Store managers make the final decision in always taking care of our customers, but we do have guidelines for matching our competition.

- We do honor "Preferred Shopping Card" advertised prices. Must be like items, be advertised, and require a competitor's shopping card, for the discount to apply.
- We do not honor advertisements that require a purchase in order to receive the advertised price or free product.
- We do not honor "Buy One / Get One Free" advertisements.
- We do not honor double or triple coupons or percent off advertisements.
- We do not honor other retailers' "Misprinted" advertised prices.
- We do not honor Internet Pricing.
- We do not honor competitor advertisements from outside of the store or Club's local trade territory.

WHOLE FOODS

Before you shop Whole Foods with coupons, here's what you should know about its policy:

- Whole Foods accepts newspaper, printable, and other manufacturer coupons.
- Whole Foods has store coupons that you can stack with a manufacturer coupon.
- Sign up for its "Whole Deal" newsletter at wholefoodsmarket.com to receive additional store coupons bi-monthly.
- Keep your eyes peeled for all sorts of coupons in store aisles. You will find tearpads, booklets, and complimentary magazines loaded with coupons.
- Take your own reusable bag to check out to save $.10 per bag.
- Consider buying the items you use most frequently, in bulk. Whole Foods will offer a discount when you buy a large quantity. Ask your customer service for more details.
- Whole Foods ads run Tuesday through Monday.
- Whole Foods is not your conventional grocery store. If you are committed to shopping organically, you may be thinking that you will be limited when it comes to shopping with coupons. Or you may be afraid your organic shopping days are over if you want to save money. While your savings will not be 70%, you can stay committed to shopping organically, all while becoming a Krazy Coupon Lady.

THE SECRET

Look for in-store coupons or store coupons from the Whole Deal newsletter to combine with a sale price. Also keep your eye out for discounted items, like meat, cheese or produce.

Example Sale: Organic Valley Cottage Cheese, $2.99
$2.00/2 from the Monthly Whole Deals Booklet
Final Price: $1.99, when you buy 2

WinCo

Before you shop WinCo with coupons, here's what you should know about its policy:

- WinCo accepts newspaper, printable, and other manufacturer coupons.
- WinCo says it follows a weekly sale schedule, but it is my finding that when something goes on sale at WinCo, the price lasts about three weeks.
- WinCo does not distribute a weekly ad or coupons on a regular basis.
- WinCo is the classic No-frills grocery store. Not a penny spent on advertising, just passing the savings on to the customer. Bag your own groceries in exchange for everyday low prices.

THE SECRET

Take your coupon binder with you whenever shopping at WinCo,
and watch for low prices and coupons to pair together!

As you peruse the aisles, watch for WinCo's initial "wall of values" and promotional pricing. Watch for things like BBQ sauce in the summer and sweetened condensed milk or soups during the winter. As WinCo prices follow the categorical sales trends, you will be able to use coupons to achieve good savings.

You will not be able to achieve savings of 70% by only shopping at a no-frills store like WinCo, but you could save $50-100 bucks a month. Compare your WinCo shopping list with TheKrazyCouponLady.com Printable Coupon Database, and print your savings before heading to the store. WinCo is meticulous about checking your printable coupons. Expect a manager to be called over to verify their validity.

WinCo can be the best place to buy some items. Dairy products tend to be priced low, and I nearly always get my soy milk free when pairing coupons with WinCo's low prices. It's just a matter of keeping your eyes peeled and doing your big stockpile shopping (like buying forty boxes of cereal for a quarter each) at a high-end store with big promotions.

Glossary

$1.00/1, $2.00/1, etc.: One dollar off one product, two dollars off one product, etc.

$1.00/2, $2.00/2, etc.: One dollar off two products, two dollars off two products, etc. You must buy two items to receive any savings; you cannot redeem the coupon on one product for half the value.

B1G1, B2G1: Another way to write "buy one, get one." The "B" stands for "buy," the "G" stands for "get." The numbers indicate how many of a product you must buy to qualify and the number of products you get when you redeem the coupon or offer. B1G1 = Buy one, get one. B2G1 = Buy two, get one. B2G2= Buy two, get two.

Blinkie: Manufacturer coupons dispensed by coupon machines found in grocery aisles next to products. Recognize them by the blinking red light. Dispenses coupons one at a time in intervals. Manufacturer blinkie coupons may be redeemed at any store, not necessarily the store in which you found them.

BOGO: Buy one, get one. Will usually end with "free" or "half off" meaning buy one, get one half off, or buy one, get one free.

Catalina: Sometimes abbreviated as "CAT," Catalina coupon machines, located at register, dispense long receipt-like coupons that may be used on a future purchase. Catalinas refer to the coupons themselves, which may be manufacturer or store coupons. Some Catalina coupons are advertised, and some are generated based on consumer behavior.

Coupon: a note from a store or manufacturer that entitles shopper to a discount on a specific product. Coupons may be clipped from the newspaper, printed from the Internet, or even downloaded to your store loyalty card.

Couponer: [koo-pon-er, kyoo-] (n.) A person who collects and saves coupons to redeem them on products, such as groceries.

Couponing: [koo-pon-ing, Kyoo-] (v.) the practice of redeeming discount coupons in order to save money.

Coupon Insert: Coupon circulars inserted into Sunday newspapers among the other advertisements. Smart Source (SS), Red Plum (RP), and Procter & Gamble (P&G) put out coupon inserts, sometimes just called "inserts." Coupon inserts are a valuable money-saving tool, and The Krazy Coupon Lady recommends buying multiple Sunday newspapers in order to have enough coupons to create a stockpile.

CRT: Cash Register Tape. Usually used when talking about CVS pharmacy, CRTs print at the bottom of your receipt and are generated based on your purchasing history (seemingly random). CRTs are specific to the store where they were printed. They are usually product specific coupons, example: $1.00 off any deodorant purchase.

Double Coupons: Select stores always double coupons up to a certain value, usually $0.50. If your store doubles coupons up to $0.50 off, any coupon $0.50 or under will be doubled in value. Coupons $0.51 or greater will be worth face value, no doubling. You do not need to present two coupons for one item. Each coupon will be worth twice the value. Other stores may double coupons on a particular week-day, usually a slower day like Tuesday. Other stores may offer physical store "twice-the-value" coupons. Even other stores may feature double coupons on a special promo week basis and will advertise this in their weekly ads.

ECB: Extra Care Buck CVS pharmacy program; now renamed Extra Bucks.

E-Coupons: Electronic coupons may be downloaded onto your store loyalty card or cell phone. Download from your PC or go mobile and download to your loyalty card through your cell phone. Grocery coupons must be downloaded to your loyalty card and will be deducted automatically when you swipe your card at checkout. E-coupons may be downloaded to your cell-phone for other retail items such as movie rentals. Download a coupon using the mobile ap and show your discount code to your cashier.

EXP: Expires or Expiration Date

Extra Bucks: CVS rewards program, formerly called ECBs. Extra Bucks print according to the store's weekly or monthly advertised deals. When you make a qualifying purchase, you receive the coordinating Extra Bucks value as advertised. Extra Bucks are similar to Catalinas or register rewards, but they print directly onto the bottom of your receipt.

FAR: Free After Rebate. Drugstores often feature a product or two that are FAR each week. An example might be Crest TotalCare toothpaste $2.49. Submit for a rebate in the amount of $2.49. This item would be considered free after rebate. You will still be responsible for sales tax.

Handling Fee: Refers to an amount, usually $0.08, paid by the manufacturer to reimburse the store for the trouble of accepting a coupon. The handling fee is usually used to pay a clearinghouse to sort, organize, and bill the manufacturer. If a store chooses to sort its own coupons, it will keep the handling fee.

IP: Internet Printable coupons may be printed right from your home computer, usually limited to two prints per computer. Download quick and safe printing software to be able to print securely from home.

IVC: Instant Value Coupon. IVCs are store coupons found in the weekly Walgreens ad. IVCs may be stacked with a manufacturer coupon.

KCL: Krazy Coupon Lady, refers to TheKrazyCouponLady.com

Krazy: Intensely enthusiastic about or preoccupied with saving money by using coupons.

Manufacturer: The company which produces the brand items: Dove soap manufacturer, Pace Salsa manufacturer, etc.

Manufacturer Coupon: A coupon created by the manufacturer, or by a marketing company on the manufacturer's behalf. Manufacturer offers a discount to shoppers in order to entice them to buy their products. When a coupon is redeemed, the manufacturer reimburses the store for the entire value of the coupon, plus a handling fee, approximately $0.08.

MFR: Manufacturer abbreviation.

MIR: Mail in Rebate, refers to rebates which must be submitted by mail. These are the traditional rebates that require you to mail in both your receipt and proof of purchase in the form of UPC barcodes.

One Coupon per Purchase: Refers to your ability to use one coupon per item. Meant to enforce the point that you may not use two of the exact same coupon for one item.

One Coupon per Transaction: Limits you to using only one of this coupon per transaction. You may request to do separate transactions. Example: If you have five coupons that read "one coupon per transaction" you may request to separate into five transactions and pay five times.

OOP: Out-of-Pocket; refers to the amount of money you will pay a store to make your purchase. Does not include after-purchase savings, coupons, or rebates.

OYNO: On Your Next Order. Store promos such as "Spend $25, save $10 on your next shopping order." OYNO refers to savings that you will not see on your first transaction, but that may be applied to your next purchase. Most OYNO coupons have no minimum purchase. If you spend $25 and receive a coupon worth $10 off your next order, there is no minimum purchase on that next order. If you spend over $10, you may redeem your coupon. If you spend under $10, you may use your coupon but will forfeit the difference.

Peelie: Adhesive manufacturer coupons found on products in the store. A peelie is often good on a wider selection of products than the one to which it is stuck. Be sure to read the fine print on the peelie to discover whether the coupon may be used on a smaller size or different variety of the same product, to allow you to maximize savings.

P&G: Procter & Gamble manufacture a wide range of consumer goods and are one of the largest corporations in the world. Procter & Gamble puts out monthly coupon inserts filled with coupons for a variety of Procter & Gamble produced brands, just a few of which include: Always, Bounty, Crest, Dawn, Gillette, Olay, Pampers, and Tide.

PSA: Prices starting at; when a group of items is on sale, such as Fiber One products 25% off. We might write "PSA $2.09" and list a group of Fiber One coupons. This means that the cheapest Fiber One product is $2.09 and prices go up from there.

Purchase: a purchase refers to buying any item. If I buy thirty items on a single shopping trip, I just made thirty purchases.

Purchase-Based Coupon: Purchase-based coupons specify a dollar amount off a minimum dollar future purchase. Some common values: $2 off $10, $3 off $15, $4 off $20. Purchase-based coupons may be used in addition to store and manufacturer coupons.

Q: Coupon abbreviation. (Not used on TheKrazyCouponLady.com).

Rain Check: A Rain Check is a written slip you can request from a store when a sale item is out of stock. When the store restocks the item, after the sale period is over, a rain check entitles you to purchase for the previous sale price. Store may include an expiration date as well as a quantity limit on your rain check. Rain checks are usually issued at the customer service desk.

Rebate: A rebate is a refund of part or all of the amount paid. KCL refers to rebates as programs that offer you cash back for making a qualified purchase. Rebates are sponsored by a store or a manufacturer. Either clip and mail UPC barcodes or enter the receipt proof of purchase online; then wait for your rebate check in the mail.

Rolling Catalinas: refers to the practice of separating your purchase into multiple transactions in order to use register Catalina coupons from your first transaction to pay for your second transaction. Another Catalina prints from the second transaction that pays for the third transaction and so on.

RP: Red Plum. Formerly known as Vallasis, Red Plum's coupon inserts and website feature coupons from a variety of manufacturers. Red Plum is part of Valassis Interactiv.

RR: Register Rewards. Walgreens drugstore rewards program, a version of the Catalina coupon. Look for the same machines located at register, dispensing long receipt-like coupons that may be used on a future purchase. RRs cannot be "rolled" like Catalinas.

SCR: Single Check Rebate, Rite Aid Drugstore monthly rebate program. Each month pick up your rebate booklet to see hundreds of dollars in possible rebate savings. Shop with coupons, save your receipts, and enter quick information online. The SCR system stores all your rebates and totals them each month. Request your monthly check be mailed to you and cash it like any other check! No clipping barcodes or UPCs, no mailing or stamping an envelope.

SS: Smart Source. A marketing company, like RP, Smart Source coupon inserts and website feature coupons from a variety of manufacturers. Smart Source is part of News America Marketing Co.

Stacking: Stacking may refer to using any two promotions together. When a coupon coincides with a promotion, we say, "stack the coupon with the sale or promotion."

Stacking Coupons: Stacking coupons refers to using both a store coupon and a manufacturer coupon on one product. Nearly all stores will allow you to "stack." Only one manufacturer coupon may be used per item.

Stockpile (n.): a food storage or stash of food and non-food items. Stockpiling is a key principle to The Krazy Coupon Lady methods. Buy items when they're on sale and you have a coupon. Buy products before you need them and build up a stockpile of food and toiletries. When you run out of an item, shop from your stockpile.

Stockpile (v.): to buy many items at a time in order to build your stockpile.

Store Coupon: A coupon created by the store to entice you to buy a certain product at that store. Stores receive no reimbursement from store coupons. Store coupons may be found in the weekly ad, printed online, or downloaded as e-coupons.

Store Loyalty Card: A free card that you present at checkout to receive additional savings. Fill out a short application to receive a loyalty card at your local grocer. If you don't want to carry the card, the cashier can look up your preferred card by entering your ten digit phone number.

Tear Pad: A pad of manufacturer coupons found near a product on shopping aisles. Tear pad manufacturer coupons may be used at any store, not just the one where you found the coupon.

Transaction: a transaction refers to your entire purchase, especially the payment you make for that purchase. If I buy thirty items and then pay the cashier, I just made one transaction.

UPC: Universal Product Code. Bar code printed on product packages that can be scanned electronically.

WAGS: Abbreviation for Walgreens Drugstore

WYB: When You Buy. Some sales or coupons require purchase of multiple items. When reporting a deal on KCL, we always include a final price. Example: Buy 2 Mint Milano cookies $2.00 each, use 2 $1.00/2 coupons, Final Price: $1.50 each, WYB 2. You must buy two in order to use the $1.00/2 coupon, so the final price states "WYB 2."

YMMV: Your Mileage May Vary. A phrase used to describe that an experience one shopper has may differ from your experience. One store may allow you to stack additional promos and another location may not do the same. Some stores, such as that "one" supercenter, that do not have a universally enforced coupon policy, will often let one customer do one thing and another do something completely different. If we receive an email from a reader with a great shopping scenario, we might report it and say, "YMMV until we see if stores nationwide are allowing the same scenario."

Index